Dedicated to the people who spend their lives striving to make the world a more hospitable place for waders.

All proceeds will go to support wader conservation through Wader Quest, a charity dedicated to the preservation and conservation of the world's waders through the passion of its volunteers.

First published in the United Kingdom by
Wader Quest Publishing 2018

Text © Rick Simpson 2018.
Line drawings © Rick Simpson 2018.
Photographs © Elis Simpson 2018.
See pages vii–x for exceptions.
Silhouette images © Elis Simpson 2018.
Maps © Adrian Riegen 2018

ISBN 978-0-9955146-1-4

Printed and bound in Great Britain by

Murrays the Printers Ltd.

An Inspiration of Waders

Twinkling gems over a falling tide

By Rick and Elis Simpson

Acknowledgements

Many people have been instrumental in my arrival at this point in my life and more particularly my involvement with waders. However, some have been more directly involved in this book than others and it is they to whom I wish to give mention here by way of thanks.

Going full circle from being influential in my initiation into birding to the present day where he has both encouraged and assisted me to write about waders is my brother Andrew. He has spent many an hour looking at my ramblings, shuffling them into some semblance of order and removing the worst offences against the English language. Likewise my parents have cast a keen eye over my prose and always encouraged my interest, even if they didn't always fully understand it, helping with indexing and initial proof reading.

Proof reading is a tremendous skill and I am particularly indebted to Brian Clews and Paul Batson for taking the time and trouble to read through the entire text and make suggestions for improvements, offering insightful, additional information. I have to thank Brian also for bringing the Ashburton coat of arms to my attention.

Obviously I also owe a great debt of gratitude to Elis, my wife who shares not only my life but my passion for waders. Rather than write about them her passion is photographing them. She is always very keen to point out she is not a bird photographer but rather a birder who likes to photograph the birds she sees. Some of her work decorates this book enhancing its visual attractiveness beyond mere words alone, and she was enthusiastic in helping me to compile the information in the first place.

Additional photos, where we do not have our own, have been kindly supplied by Julian Bhalerao, Mike Bridgeford, Ric Else, Knut Hansen, Matt Jones, John Kinghorn and Niall Perrins.

Thanks too to the staff at the British Natural History Museum Bird Collection at Tring Museum, in particular Mark Adams, for access to the skin collection.

Many people have encouraged me to write this book, among them Keith Betton and Dominic Couzens, both of whom made me believe it was worth doing. Thanks are also due to Keith for writing the foreword supporting our own view that waders are wonderful and deserve our admiration.

Part of the book is about other people and how waders inspired them and changed their lives. I thank all contributors for kindly sharing their stories with me and allowing me to share them with you, they are; Richard Chandler, Rob Clay, Mary Colwell, Alexia Fishwick, Patricia González, Astrid Kant, Karen Leeming, Clive Minton, Theunis Piersma, Oliver Simms, Pavel

Tomkovich, David Turner, and Yvonne Verkuil.

Some stories come from people we have met and yet others from those we have not met. Thank you to Robin Diaz and Alice van Zoeren (piping plover), John Dowding (shore plover), Patricia González (Moonbird), Cody Thyne and Jemma Welch (black stilts), Lin Zhiang (snipe and clam) for sharing these stories with us. Thanks also to Lucy Grove for letting us use part of her '*A Shropshire Curlew*' poem and Inge van der Zee of *Bond Friese VogelWachten* (BFVW) for her help with the Friesland lapwing egg collecting tradition.

The excellent maps which enhance Chapter 6 have come from Adrian Riegen in New Zealand. I wrote to ask permission to use one he had previously produced and he then offered to make the others specifically for this book, which was much appreciated.

Chapter headings have some quotes with splendid words written about waders. Some of the authors are no longer with us and I thank them posthumously; Sven Waxell, Charles Dixon, Peter Matthiessen, Kenneth Richmond, and Herbert Brandt. But there are those that are happily still with us and have kindly allowed us to quote them, they are; Matt Merritt, Michael O'Brien, Richard Crossley and Kevin Karlson.

Lastly I'd like to thank Jaffa, our indoor cat, for being there when I needed to talk about ideas, which I didn't want any argument over, and to de-stress when it seemed, as it often did, all too much like hard work - even though she slept through most of it.

Contents

Acknowledgements   i

Foreword   Keith Betton   xiii

Preface   xvii

An inspiring attempt to define waders   xxiii

Chapter 1   A young boy inspired   1

Chapter 2   Others inspired   9

Chapter 3   Inspiring art and literature   33

Chapter 4   Inspiring myths and legends   49

Chapter 5   Inspiring miscellany   77

Chapter 6   Inspirational waders   91

Chapter 7   An inspiration of waders   107

Appendix I   Collective nouns of waders   115

Appendix II   Spoony ditty   125

Appendix III   About Wader Quest   131

List of Silhouettes
(Elis Simpson)

Dedication   Eurasian stone-curlew, common redshank, common ringed plover & Eurasian whimbrel.

Title page   A mixed flight of waders.

Spacer in text   Diademed sandpiper-plover.

List of Illustrations
(Rick Simpson)

page   i   Spoon-billed sandpiper.

page   xiii   Hooded plover.

page   xvii   Red-necked phalarope.

page   xxiii   Buff-breasted sandpiper.

page   1   Common greenshank and common redshank.

page   9   Dunlin being ringed.

page   33   Lapwing hieroglyph.

page   49   Egyptian plover and crocodile.

page   77   Killdeer.

page   91   Rocky the piping plover.

page   107   An inspiration and waders on an estuary.

page   115   Sociable and northern lapwing in flight.

page   125   Spoon-billed sandpiper.

page   131   Black-winged stilt.

page   139   White-rumped sandpiper.

page   147   Common greenshank.

List of Photographs

All photographs by **Elis Simpson** unless otherwise stated.

Front cover — An inspiration of waders over the Snettisham shore; Norfolk, England.

page v — Broad-billed sandpiper.

page xi — Andean avocet.

page xii — *Top to bottom/left to right*: Northern lapwing; red-kneed dotterel; red-capped plover; red-necked stint; Eurasian stone-curlew; Javan Lapwing (**©The Trustees of the Natural History Museum, London**); Eskimo curlew and slender-billed curlew (both **©The Trustees of the Natural History Museum, London**); black stilt; southern red-breasted plover (**Matt Jones**); sociable lapwing; spoon-billed sandpiper; shore plover.

page xv — A layer cake of waders over the Wash; Norfolk, England.

page xxi — Comb-crested jacana.

page xxii — *Top to bottom/left to right*: Wattled jacana; South American painted-snipe; crab plover; Magellanic oystercatcher; ibisbill; white-backed stilt; water thick-knee; Magellanic plover; rock pratincole; black-fronted dotterel; Egyptian plover; little stint; least seedsnipe; snowy sheathbill (**Mike Bridgeford**); plains wanderer (**Niall Perrins**); common buttonquail (**John Kinghorn**).

page xxix — Northern lapwing.

page xxx — *Top to bottom/left to right*: Common redshank; common greenshank; grey plover; ruddy turnstone; sanderling; stilt sandpiper; little curlew (**Ric Else**); spoon-billed sandpiper.

page 7   Double-banded courser with chick.
page 8   *Top to bottom/left to right*: Red knot; black-
                tailed godwit; buff-breasted sandpiper; green
                sandpiper; American golden plover; solitary
                sandpiper; white-rumped sandpiper; ruff.
page 31   Spotted redshank.
page 32   *Top to bottom/left to right*: Grey
                phalarope; purple sandpiper; Eurasian
                curlew; dunlin; Eurasian oystercatcher;
                Eurasian woodcock (**Julian Bhalerao**);
                wandering tattler; common snipe.
page 47   Little ringed plover.
page 48   *Top to bottom/left to right*: Egyptian
                plover; spur-winged lapwing; white-headed
                stilt; red-wattled lapwing; Eurasian
                dotterel; Pacific golden plover; Eurasian
                whimbrel; European golden plover.
page 75   Black-winged stilt.
page 76   *Top to bottom/left to right*: American
                woodcock (**Knut Hansen**); pied avocet;
                common ringed plover; killdeer; curlew
                sandpiper; pectoral sandpiper; sharp-tailed
                sandpiper; common sandpiper.
page 89   Bar-tailed godwit (*baueri*).
page 90   *Top to bottom/left to right*: Shore plover OG
                -YR; wrybill; red-necked phalarope (**Julian
                Bhalerao**); Rocky the piping plover; black
                stilt; semipalmated plover; mountain plover;
                snowy plover.
page 105   Surfbird.
page 106   An inspiration of waders over the Snettisham
                shore; Norfolk, England.
page 113   An inspiration of waders.
page 114   A fling of dunlins.
page 123   An incontinence of yellowlegs.
page 124   Spoon-billed sandpiper.

page 129   Hooded plover.
page 130   *Top to Bottom:* Western sandpiper;
                  semipalmated sandpiper; Baird's sandpiper.
page 137   River lapwing.
page 138   Our library.
page 145   Puna plover.
page 146   Spotted thick-knee.

List of Maps

All maps by **Adrian Riegen**.

page 103   E7 Bar-tailed Godwit migration route.
page 104   B95 Moonbird red knot migration route.
                  Red-necked phalarope migration route.

Foreword by Keith Betton

Waders are wonderful!

Yes - waders really are wonderful! For me, they surpass all other bird families in so many ways. Their physical adaptations, their ability to migrate, their nesting strategies, and the way that they cope with what appears to be quite a stressful life – are all things that endear them to me.

Just from a physical standpoint, waders are brilliantly adapted with beaks that can be long or short, upturned or down-curved (and even sideways). They work out strategies to feed when food is available regardless of the time of day. If there is a full moon, northern lapwings will choose to feed by night for several days to take advantage of the extra light. Waders also move rapidly to avoid cold weather or take advantage of good feeding opportunities. For example, red-kneed dotterels and the red-capped plovers make large-scale movements to and from areas in Australia with heavy rainfall.

Most waders migrate between breeding and wintering areas and some do so on a truly global scale. Consider the huge journeys from the Arctic to Australia for the bar-tailed godwit and red-necked stint, which are undertaken in just a few weeks. These birds can double their body mass in just two months to ensure they are able to make these huge journeys.

When they arrive at their breeding grounds most waders are masters at hiding their nests and young, and when attacked some, such as northern lapwings, are terrific at working as a group to see off predators. I have the privilege of studying Eurasian stone-curlews in the United Kingdom, and I never cease to be amazed at how they hide their nests and try to make me think that they have nested in a different part of a field!

The conservation of our waders is of vital importance and the work of Wader Quest in highlighting on-going threats is to be applauded. Already gone are three species that have vanished within living memory - Javan lapwing, Eskimo curlew and slender-billed curlew. Others such as black stilt, southern red-breasted plover, sociable lapwing and spoon-billed sandpiper are on the Critically Endangered list, while several more species are declining and need our attention. Some have wide distributions and are hard to focus on, while others, such as the shore plover have a tiny world distribution of just a few square kilometres.

Even if breeding populations are thriving, waders are at greater risk than most species from the effects of Global Climate Change. Sea levels monitored by satellite have shown a rise of seven centimetres in just the last twenty-five years. As the water rises, so the areas where waders feed and roost are reduced. Schemes that we create to protect ourselves from these sea-level rises in turn often reduce wader habitats. When waders choose to roost inland because of the changes they are often disturbed by people who want to use such areas for recreation. It feels as if the threats are never-ending. My message is clear – let's take good care of our waders.

I am delighted to welcome this book, as it is a celebration of the historical, cultural and aesthetic connections that we all have with waders.

Indeed, anything that raises awareness of waders and makes people appreciate them more is to be welcomed. Enjoy this book for the stories it tells about waders in our lives and how we have celebrated them through art, poetry, music and storytelling. Enjoy their plumages, from those with bright colours to others that use incredible camouflage to avoid detection. And if you can, please go out and watch waders. Enjoy the spectacle of thousands of them swirling around the sky like sections in a multi-layered cake (see below) – and more than anything, enjoy waders for being an inspiration to us all.

Keith Betton is a media trainer, PR consultant and writer. He is a keen world birder having seen over 8,200 species including all but 20 wader species. He has a passion for Africa and the Middle East, having been Chairman of both the African Bird Club and the Ornithological Society of the Middle East (OSME). In the UK he is heavily involved in bird monitoring in Hampshire, where he is County Recorder. A former Council Member of both the Royal Society for the Protection of Birds (RSPB) and the British Trust for Ornithology (BTO), he is currently Vice President of the latter.

Preface

Although this offering does not purport to be an exhaustive account of humanity's relationship with waders, it does chart how this most varied family of birds has inspired us over the centuries, from cave paintings onwards.

These pages explain both my own development as a birder and the influence waders have had upon my life as well as how they have influenced other individuals, affecting their lives in a variety of ways. How waders have been depicted and described is also discussed, looking at some of the characteristics that we have bestowed upon them through observation and indeed ignorance much of the time.

There are few facets of human culture that have not been affected in some way by waders. We depict them in art, we write songs and poems about them, we study them and eulogise about them. We have created myths and legends to explain the unexplainable, drawing them into our lives and using them as foils, villains and heroes, some to be dismissed as gun fodder while others may be placed among the gods. They are beautiful, graceful and entertaining, but their elevated status is not born purely of our imaginings; they have proved themselves to be among the most resilient species in the world of birds with extraordinary feats of endurance. The mere fact that they still survive, despite everything that we have done to thwart their continued existence, bears witness to their hardiness and tenacity, which merit our awe and admiration.

These inspiring birds are on the wane. They are losing the battle for survival, largely due to the obstacles they face to reproduce, be it on the breeding ground itself or elsewhere influencing whether they return from their migration in good enough condition to breed, or even at all.

A world without waders is unthinkable. They have been so important in our lives, as this selection of facts and stories hopefully illustrates, and it is surely time that we acknowledge the part they have played in making our lives that much richer, returning the favour, by ensuring they also have a future.

Waders do not require culture, art or any of the foibles of human nature: all they require is a level playing field and a chance to go about their lives unhindered. We can go a long way to providing at least an element of interspecies equitability, simply by removing some of the barriers to survival that we are erecting in every environment in which this eclectic bunch of birds dwell.

The final chapter of this book highlights one of the most inspiring of nature's phenomena; the spectacle of a mass flight of waders, those twinkling gems over a falling tide, which hitherto have not had an adequate collective noun to describe them. Taking into account everything that is written beforehand in the preceding chapters we suggest a collective noun for this natural, untamed and exuberant exhibition of precision which is carried out, often unnoticed and unwatched, every day somewhere on our planet.

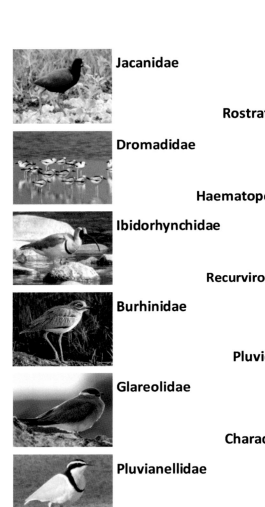

Jacanidae

Rostratulidae

Dromadidae

Haematopodidae

Ibidorhynchidae

Recurvirostridae

Burhinidae

Pluvionidae

Glareolidae

Charadriidae

Pluvianellidae

Scolopacidae

Thinocoridae

Chionidae

Pedionomidae

Turnicidae

An inspired attempt to define waders

Here, at the very outset, in the name of clarity, we should define exactly what we mean by waders, or at least try.

Traditionally they have been described as being medium-sized birds with long legs and bills, possessing a sombre, grey-brown plumage, sometimes with black and or white patches. They are birds of coastal and inland water margins and often form into flocks in the non-breeding season. Whilst these are all typical, they are by no means exclusive, complete or even constant characteristics.

In scientific terms all life forms are classified into kingdom, phylum, class, order, family, genus, species and, in some cases, subspecies. In the case of waders, we are referring to the species of bird to be found within the sub-order Charadrii, itself to be found in the order Charadriifomes, as defined in the seminal *Shorebirds* book of 1986. At that time the group of species encompassed within the suborder

Charadrii were in the following families;

Jacanidae	jacanas
Rostratulidae	painted-snipes
Dromadidae	crab plover
Haematopodidae	oystercatchers
Ibidorhynchidae	ibisbill
Recurvirostridae	stilts and avocets
Burhinidae	stone-curlews and thick-knees
Glareolidae	pratincoles and coursers
Charadriidae	lapwings, dotterels and plovers
Pluvianellidae	Magellanic plover
Scolopacidae	godwits, curlews, whimbrels, shanks, sandpipers, tattlers, turnstones, phalaropes, snipes, woodcocks, dowitchers and stints
Thinocoridae	seedsnipes

Since that time the Egyptian plover has been split from the pratincoles and coursers into a family of its own;

Pluvionidae	Egyptian plover

Taxonomy is not always universally accepted and even back then some authors, including those of the 1964 *The New Dictionary of Birds* also included;

Chionidae	sheathbills

This then is the group we understood to be waders for a considerable period of time, with the extreme ends - jacanas, seedsnipes and sheathbills - being a little bit of a stretch of the imagination for some.

Things got stretched still further with the addition of a species to the suborder that did not immediately seem to fit the genre. The *Handbook of Birds of the World* Vol 3. (1996) included;

Pedionomidae   plains wanderer

This seemed to be a strange thing to include as its outward resemblance to the other waders was miniscule. However more recently the addition of a family of birds which seems to fit neatly alongside the plains wanderer made it less obtrusive, but their inclusion has complicated the definition of this suborder still further they are;

Turnicidae   buttonquails

Whatever you do, or don't, include in this group, whether you actually call this subset of birds waders or not depends to a large extent upon where you were when you learnt about birds.

What we refer to as waders in the UK our good friends on the other side of the Atlantic Ocean, and perhaps elsewhere in the English speaking world, might prefer to refer to as shorebirds.

The words 'wader' and 'shorebird' are synonymous in this context. One is not better than the other, both are widely used where English is spoken, are interchangeable, and refer to the same group of birds (whatever your definition of that is). In *The New Dictionary of Birds* 'wader' was considered British and 'shorebird' the North American version of the same thing. But, like so much of our language these days 'Americanisms' have crossed the Atlantic via films, TV, books and social media. Many words and phrases that you simply would not have heard in the UK are now commonplace, among them the use of 'shorebird' to mean 'wader'.

If you look at the full title of the great pioneering identification guide for this group of birds you will notice that it is *Shorebirds: An identification guide to the waders of the world;* Messrs. Hayman, Marchant and Prater hedging their bets a little there; perhaps with a weathered eye on the greater potential market that the US provides?

This is all well and good except that it can cause some confusion in that each word can very well mean something different to those that are not familiar with their synonymy in this specific use. One can, for example, find people who refer to shorebirds and will include within that definition terns, gulls, ducks and geese, and not unreasonably either, since they are birds that frequent the shore. On the other hand some will refer to waders and include within that herons, egrets, ibises and spoonbills, even rails, in fact any bird that wades, and once again quite reasonably.

This same group of birds was formerly known scientifically as Limicolae, meaning 'mud dwellers' which is perhaps rather more apt than either 'wader' or 'shorebird' as most species are associated with mud in some way, be it dry or wet, for a great deal of their annual cycle; phalaropes being something of an exception here. However suitable 'mud birds' might be to describe these birds, it is unlikely that it will overturn the decades of traditional 'wader' and 'shorebird' use. In any case, a great many other birds dwell on mud in addition to these.

How then do we define waders? What sets them apart? Which characteristic do they all share that no other birds share? Unfortunately the answer is none really. Apart from the classics (sandpipers and plovers) some families at the fringes of the sub-order look like gallinules (jacanas) and others like grouse (seedsnipes). Frustratingly there is no single thing that captures them, barring all others. Some commentators have referred to the Charadrii as being a waste-basket taxa, somewhere to fit things that don't seem to fit anywhere else and that don't necessarily fit together either. Perhaps it is time to invent a name, to coin a new word that fits them all? Despite much cogitation on this issue in an attempt to find a suitable alternative, the fact remains that the variety of species now included in this group of birds defies easy definition within a single word.

Back in the early days of the colonisation of the Americas in North America these birds were referred to as 'bay birds' or 'bay snipes', once again referring to the original group of birds that do indeed wade in water or remain very near to it, before the confusing array of other types were added to their number. In the end, we will probably continue to use both 'wader' and 'shorebird' across the world in English speaking lands, and for the most part, we will be reasonably well understood among those that care.

The great variety of waders in terms of physical attributes is another reason we are unable to pin them down to find a universal word for them. Many have long legs suitable for wading through water or long grass while others have very short legs; some feed in the water, some on dry land and some even feed on the wing; some waders have membranes between their toes called webs, some none, yet others will have a combination of both and some even have feet that resemble a coot; there are extremes of toe length too, some extremely long and some very short, some have fully functioning hind toes, some vestigial hind toes and some none at all. One thing all waders do have in common is that they all run or walk and do not hop in order to get around on the ground. An exception to this is when they are asleep, standing on one leg when, if pushed to do so they will, rather endearingly, hop to avoid whatever has disturbed them in preference to dropping their second leg to walk or run. Purple Sandpipers and other rock loving waders also hop between rocks at times but on a level surface they will always walk.

The bills of waders can be long, medium or short, they come straight or curved - either upwards or downwards and in one case sideways; there is one with a spoon-shaped bill. Some bills are narrow, some are broad and this wide variety exists due to a particular feeding niche that each species fills. Tail shape and the number of feathers therein varies as does the relative length and shape of wings. Some birds are highly migratory, others are not and the distribution of waders is worldwide.

Summing up this varied collection of birds succinctly and unanimously, in one word or indeed a phrase, while eliminating all other birds appears impossible. We will use the term 'waders' for the purposes of this book and the birds included are those listed on page xxiv and xxv above.

Chapter One

A young boy inspired

'A group of around two hundred golden plovers flash and spangle in the last of the sun, performing their strange alchemy with every turn. At first they're dark, indistinct dots, before, banking left, they brighten into little white-hot ingots, finally turning again and falling as a rain of gold pieces... All of this has me, for a moment, quite forgetting where I am.'

A Sky Full of Birds (2016) - Matt Merritt

One cold, wet and windy school holiday afternoon in the early 1960s, a small boy came across a striking image in a bird book that his brother owned. It was of a northern lapwing, a bird with which he was not familiar, indeed he'd never even heard of it before. Back in those days of course they didn't bother with the 'northern' bit, it was simply labelled lapwing. With the impetuosity of youth (and worrying indications for a future twitching career) he immediately wanted to see one but, as these were not garden birds, this was something of a forlorn hope. Even though this was before 'bucket lists' had been invented, he made seeing a lapwing a must-do priority in his life. It turns out that, in this instance, his impatience could be assuaged as his brother knew just where to find a flock nearby and he promised to take him to see them.

That small boy was me, and upon seeing the birds in real life, even at a distance and without any optics, I was captivated by the way they ran around the field randomly, completely independent of each other as though in their own little world. However, when something disturbed them, they went up as one and flew around in a cohesive group with a bouncy flight, which I found entrancing. I was also smitten by their British racing green backs, from which they derived the old name of green plover, blending them seamlessly into the British countryside. I further enjoyed the comical noises they made as they flew and was amused by another vernacular name for them, peewit, which derived from those calls, and I resolved to use it henceforth. I had been made aware that birds existed and had developed a passing interest in them, but these birds had something special and they greatly excited my young mind, kick-starting my life-long love of birds and, in particular, waders.

The same brother was further responsible for my increased appreciation of waders when at our primary school he created a marvellous painting of a common redshank and a common greenshank together on the shoreline. This artwork was of sufficient quality for it to be put on display at London's Natural History Museum before being returned to our school. The teaching staff deemed it worthy of being placed on the wall of the school hall so each assembly thereafter, until it was removed, I sat and contemplated that painting with a mixture of envy and admiration. Heaven knows how much moral guidance I missed whilst absorbing every aspect of that picture of two birds that I had never seen; I closely observed the differences between the two whilst noting their obvious similarities. It was the beginning of my long and, as yet, far from complete journey along the road of wader identification.

Actually, it turns out the 'bucket list' alluded to wasn't such a stretch of the imagination after all. In my teens, it was waders that very nearly lured me to a sticky end. I encountered my first ruddy turnstones, sanderlings and grey plovers on a memorable day in Essex. The ruddy turnstones were in their breeding finery, as was one of the grey plovers puffing out its proud, black chest for me to admire. The sanderlings moved in an amusing way with such energy that they further kindled my growing passion for waders of all kinds. The day was memorable though, not just for those inspirational birds that fed my adolescent imagination, but also because it might well have turned out to be my last day on earth. As I ventured ever closer, concentrating on getting better views of these new and stunning birds, my feet became inextricably embedded in the cloying ooze. Try as I might I could not liberate myself from the mud and eventually, in panic, my rubber boots were abandoned to be consumed by the mire and swallowed by the incoming tide as I scrambled for safety discovering, the hard way, that being a wader was not as easy as it looks. It was also the day I resolved to buy a telescope when I could afford one.

During my inevitable twitching years, the birds I found the most alluring and irresistible were the vagrant waders. Give me a stilt sandpiper over a Swainson's thrush any day! I was positively beside myself when I found myself watching a hopelessly displaced wader that was then known as little whimbrel, now little curlew, in Norfolk that should have been on its way to the other side of the world.

Fast forward to the present – my enthusiasm for waders has remained with me and indeed has infected my long suffering wife Elis (beware, waders may be a contagious obsession) compelling us to establish Wader Quest, our own charity dedicated to wader conservation. This started with the news that the spoon-billed sandpiper was heading towards extinction. In the 1990s I had missed my chance to see slender-billed curlew and this troubled me greatly. Having let one enigmatic wader species slip into oblivion without my seeing one, I was not about to let it happen again.

During our preparations to see this bird, Elis and I were attended a talk given by Nigel Clark, then of the BTO, explaining why the bird was in such a parlous state, dramatically altering our outlook and compelling us to think about some way in which we might be able to help.

In all truth there was really only one way that we could reasonably be of any value and that would be as fundraisers. We decided we would raise money for the spoon-billed sandpiper captive breeding programme at Slimbridge Wildfowl and Wetlands Trust (WWT) and the way we would do it would be to travel the world, at our own expense I hasten to add, to see as many wader species as possible in one year. This we hoped would capture the imaginations of the bird loving public who would then donate to our crowd-funding site, building a sizeable donation for the WWT and the spoonies.

During those travels yet more enlightenment came in the form of discovering just how many species, in a wide variety of habitats, were also suffering from the cavalier attitude humanity has towards the environment. Birds that utterly depend on certain sets of conditions to survive found that these were being compromised where they breed, where they pass the non-breeding season and, if they are migrants, all along the flyways in between.

In the end our fundraising wasn't hugely successful, we were a bit naïve when it came to promoting the event, many of those that heard about us thought they'd be paying for our travel and I'm not sure the WWT thought our efforts were going to amount to much either. As a result, it didn't end up being the fundraiser we had hoped, managing to raise just £3,526.06.

The most significant thing to come from those trips though was the growing realisation that wader conservation is not just about one species with a funny beak in the far flung corners of Asia. It is, due to the worldwide distribution of waders, a global problem that pertains to every habitat in which waders are found.

Our first lesson in this respect unexpectedly came early in our adventures. On November the 1st 2012 Elis and I set off for Norfolk from our home in Northamptonshire on the first day of our Wader Quest project. We had hoped to get off to a flying start in the UK on this first morning before jetting off around the world. The bird which we both thought most likely to take the honour of being the first on our list was northern lapwing. We had every reason to be confident of this prediction as we would be driving across The Fens, an area of countryside eminently suitable for them. It seemed inconceivable that we would fail in this endeavour even though there is not much left of what could realistically be labelled Fenland these days - most of it having been drained and replaced by acres of peat rich farmland. To our surprise, and utter dismay, we failed completely, but not for the want of trying I can assure you. We arrived at Titchwell without seeing a single lapwing along the way.

Although it was perhaps a little early for large flocks of northern lapwings to have assembled for the winter, not seeing any at all was perplexing. This episode served as a blunt reminder that Britain's most common wader, our beloved northern lapwing, had declined by eighty per cent, particularly in southern England and Wales, since the days when I was a lad peddling off to see my first. The place in which I first saw them, some fields near to our home on the Hertfordshire-Middlesex border, has changed beyond recognition. Most of the fields which then catered for these birds are now long gone, having been replaced by housing developments or significantly degraded as suitable lapwing breeding habitat by drainage and changing farming practices, and therein lies the story behind the bird's decline.

As we travelled the globe we came across bays that were to be dredged to create marinas for the rich and famous to moor their opulent yachts. We saw a double-banded courser breeding ground turned into a quad bike circuit. We found agricultural fields where previously there had been wetlands and we observed mudflats and beaches being turned over to alternative uses such as industry, housing, aquaculture and intensive human recreation that further diminished the breeding and foraging possibilities for our waders.

Once we had finished our travelling we realised that we couldn't simply leave it there, Wader Quest morphed into the charity it is today motivated by what we had discovered during our journeys in search of waders.

Chapter Two

Others inspired

'The restlessness of shorebirds their kinship with the distance and swift seasons, the wistful signal of their voices down the long coastlines of the world make them the most affecting of wild creatures.'

The Wind Birds (1973) - Peter Matthiessen (1927-2014)

It is not just Elis and I who have been inspired by waders though, we are far from unique. When first confronted, waders can be a difficult group of birds to get enthusiastic about. However, once they have got under your skin, what starts as a flirtatious infatuation can soon develop into something rather more overwhelming - abiding love.

People who are new to birdwatching can find waders a bit daunting if identifying them is the only goal. But if experiencing a more general appreciation of them is allowed, then waders take on a whole different perspective.

Two people who have expressed this to us have been a

young man called Oliver and a young lady called Alexia. Both wrote articles for the Wader Quest newsletter outlining how they had become interested in waders. In Oliver's case it was as he was taking the first tentative steps into birdwatching, he went to look at a wader scrape and was captivated by what he saw. The wealth and variety of the birds he encountered, with waders evident in every direction, drew him in and he was hooked. He entitled his piece '*Waders with the power to Inspire'*. Alexia's experience was slightly different as it was a wader roost that caught her attention. Wader roosts really are once-seen-never-forgotten experiences and they cannot be imagined until they have been witnessed first-hand. The breath-taking excitement that the birds arouse by their impressive aerobatics and the thrill of seeing such sheer numbers of birds together in one place, leave a lasting impression. Alexia's title? *'Inspired by my first Wader Roost'*.

There are a number of well respected, if not revered, 'waderologists', people, both professional and amateur, who study waders with a view to improving wader conservation and increasing the chances of their survival. These are often perceived to be strictly scientific people who tend to look at the world in a less romantic way than the rest of us non-scientifically trained folk. To debunk this idea we asked some of our friends in the wader world how they became enamoured of waders to demonstrate that they too are in possession of the same human emotions as the rest of us when it comes to the waders they study; they all have individual stories to tell about how they became devoted to waders.

One such person is Theunis Piersma, a Dutch professor of Global Flyway Ecology at the University of Groningen in the Netherlands. Theunis describes himself as a man of open landscapes where waders are a phenomenon that is hard to ignore. He wrote to tell us;

'What intrigued me from the start, and led me to seriously devote my attention to waders (at the age of 18, as a beginning biology student at the University of Groningen), was this idea that waders all but encircle the globe as individuals, knitting the magnificent open landscapes together. That awe has never left me, and what has grown is a deep feeling for their beauty as individuals, as flocks, and in their performances. Waders are a bit of an acquired taste, but it is a lovely taste to have acquired when it is satisfied, and a painful one in the face of the worldwide rampant destruction of the habitats that they (and we!) depend upon.'

Theunis' admiration for these birds has manifested itself in a profusion of works and books, the latest of which, *Marathon Migrants* summarises his love and admiration for waders. Much of Theunis' work has been devoted to studying the red knot and he has the well-deserved honour of having a subspecies named after him; *Calidris canutus piersmai*.

Another Dutch ornithologist, Yvonne Verkuil, has been the Chair of the International Wader Study Group (IWSG) for ten years, a post to which she is eminently suited. She has carried out this role ably and with enthusiasm alongside her professional career working with waders at the University of Groningen with a six year stint (if you'll pardon the pun) at the

Royal Ontario Museum in Toronto Canada. This total immersion in the world of waders, their study and conservation, over a prolonged period of time, is a manifestation of her dedication and passion for this intriguing group of birds. When asked how this had come about, this was her reply;

'I like to be asked why I'm fascinated by waders and how that started. Because the question makes me relive the evening in 1990 on a (then) very remote island that changed my life. There, on Griend in the middle of the Wadden Sea in mid-January, I received my maiden training in field work on waders, following red knots and sampling mudflats. It was cold, wet, stormy, and the housing was very primitive, but we were prepared and I loved every second of it. What I was not prepared for, was the flock of thirty thousand red knots one evening wanting to settle on the island for high tide, but being undecided for a long time while the sun was setting. Now I have seen such scenes many times, but then I was unprepared and completely overwhelmed, and I fell in love, deeply and hopelessly.'

That same year she joined the Wader Study Group which later became what is now the IWSG, where she felt immediately at home. She continues:

'I have been a proud member of the shorebird community ever since. Almost eighteen years later it was proposed that I would take over the Chair position in the IWSG, I felt very honoured and immediately motivated, especially because many people in the executive committee had become my friends.'

Disarmingly Yvonne suggests that working with friends does not feel like work at all, somewhat diminishing her hard work and achievements. She did nevertheless find that, in common with many executive committee members, running the IWSG was a perfect training ground for a professional career with waders. Again with modesty she concluded;

'I feel the Group has given me more than I have ever invested, and the kind, collaborative attitude of wader people around the world is keeping me motivated.'

It must have been at least thirty years ago that another Dutch lady, Astrid Kant, fell in love with the black-tailed godwit. As a young girl she became interested in animals and in particular birds. She had a soft spot for sick or injured animals that needed help, turning her bedroom into an animal hospital.

At the age of twenty-two she bought a house in the middle of the Netherlands in the green heart of Holland. She found herself surrounded by vast green meadows full of grass, an enormous number of cows and many godwits, which she found enchanting.

But things have not stayed idyllic for Astrid or the godwits. Farming methods have changed from mowing flower-strewn meadows in mid-June after the godwits had fledged, to silage meadows which are mowed earlier, even as early as April. This has had dire consequences for the godwits. Those chicks that were not killed directly by the mowers were easily picked off by predators as they tried to flee. As the godwit population started to decline, Astrid could not stand by and watch. She was impelled to do something about the situation. She says;

'A good healthy godwit population needs healthy big chicks not omelettes!'

Astrid started to engage with the farmers; talking to them, laughing and crying with them and most of all trying to train them to be aware of the godwits' needs.

'We are birdwatchers' she said *'they are farmers. You can't expect them to know the breeding ecology of the godwits.'*

And she was right, the first farmer she visited was utterly mystified by her assertion that he had godwits nesting on his land;

'How can I have godwit nests on my land?' he asked in all seriousness *'I don't have any trees!'*

It was going to be an uphill battle to overcome such lack of knowledge but one incident hardened Astrid's resolve to continue.

'Twenty years ago I found and marked a lot of godwit nests at a particular farm, later that week the farmer mowed his fields and the meadows were horribly quiet; no more godwit sounds. But there in the drying grass I saw a female godwit apparently incubating. I wondered what was going on. As I approached I heard the chirping of some chicks and, under the sitting bird, beneath the mown grass, I found four one day old chicks still in the nest. Two of them were dead, one was missing its legs and one was still alive, apparently unharmed.'

With a heavy heart Astrid despatched the injured bird and felt wretched; she had missed a nest and now had been forced to kill a chick as a result. This was the moment that she decided to take action and raise awareness about the miserable story that was unfolding around her. She was further inspired to write a book called *Weidevogels* (Meadow Birds) in which she relates the trials, tribulations and perils of being a godwit on a modern Dutch farm. She also gives many talks and lectures to farmers and volunteers.

Astrid spends many hours in the field every spring, to which we can attest as we were privileged to spend a weekend with her one year. She visits most of her thirty farmers at least five times, protecting up to two hundred and fifty godwit families. As a result her godwit population is bucking the trend and increasing. Recently she received an award from the King of the Netherlands in honour of the work she does as guardian of the godwits but she says her greatest reward is her increasing godwit population.

Russian Ornithologist and co-author of the *Atlas of Breeding Waders in the Russian Arctic*, Pavel Tomkovich, told us that he has been interested in wildlife since childhood. He suggests this is partly due to his mother being a biology teacher although he became especially interested in birds, rather than plants or other animals, after reading a number of popular books by Russian scientists such as Vitaly Bianki and Eugeny Spangenberg. His special interest in waders sprung from a visit to the Indigirka River area in the Siberian tundra in 1972 as an undergraduate student in the Moscow State University under Professor Vladimir Flint. Pavel wrote;

'Following the advice of Professor Flint my diploma research became a study of the comparative breeding biology of pectoral and sharp-tailed sandpipers. Seeing an impressive diversity of wader species in the Siberian tundra, as well as a diversity of their breeding systems in the same general environment, along with a gradual realisation of how poorly the various aspects of their lives, especially those of Siberian

endemics, were known, made me stick with waders, mostly Calidris sandpipers, for the rest of my life.'

Since late 1976, when he became a researcher at the Zoological Museum of Moscow State University, his dreams have become a reality as this presented him with opportunities to learn about specialisations of various tundra wader species – their differences, adaptations, distribution, population structure, history, etc.

Rob Clay is the Director of the Western Hemisphere Shorebird Reserve Network (WHSRN - pronounced 'Wissen') Executive Office based in Paraguay. For as long as he can remember, birds, and in particular water birds, have been an important part of his life. He grew up in the vicinity of Langstone Harbour with Farlington Marshes as his second home, and, he tells us, was strongly influenced by his father George Clay, a keen birdwatcher.

'Thus, my early years as a birder were spent with Dad who was part of the original 'Portsmouth Group', and first visited Farlington Marshes in 1949. I was immersed in his anecdotes and birding diary entries about waders in the local area (and how their numbers had changed over the decades). As a young birder struggling to identify waders by sight, I can vividly recall Dad teaching me their calls, as we walked home from Farlington Marshes one night. To this day, every time I hear a grey plover it brings back that memory. My weekends were spent watching waders in the local estuaries, with the occasional twitch (one of the first, when I was only seven, being for a buff-breasted sandpiper), while walks to school entailed searches for green

sandpipers on the local stream.'

Thanks to his parents' support, he was able to pursue a career in ornithology, which led him to the Neotropics, and initially forest bird conservation.

'However, I soon discovered that Asunción Bay on the Paraguay River was an important stopover site for waders, and in particular buff-breasted sandpipers. This was the first step in a path to a career focused on wader conservation, but which has also enabled me to go 'full circle' and teach my son wader identification by call (albeit American golden plovers and solitary sandpipers).'

Another very prominent waderologist in South America is Argentinian scientist Patricia González, who worked closely with the Late Dr Allan Baker, an eminent member of the wader research community.

In 1995, Dr Baker organised an expedition to Tierra del Fuego during which the team placed a plain orange flag and two colour bands on the red knots they caught. In 2001, a follow-up expedition was carried out during which experimental, inscribed flags were placed on red knots for the first time. Birds that had not previously been caught were given flags with the letter A followed by two numbers. Birds that had previously been caught in 1995 had their plain flags removed and new ones, sporting the letter B and two numbers, put on them instead.

Patricia took part in both expeditions, and it was she who placed the ring bearing the number B95 on what was to become the most famous red knot in the world, Moonbird (the story of which can be seen in chapter six). Years later she realised the number was very fitting as the B recognised the organiser of the expeditions, Dr Baker, and the 95 represented the year Moonbird had first been ringed, possibly also by Patricia, although no-one really knows.

Birds, however, had not featured in Patricia's early life. In contrast to so many other people mentioned in this chapter, she has been converted, not by the gentle persuasion of a fellow enthusiast, but by the birds themselves and a pair of binoculars.

'Birds never caught my attention!' she admitted. Upon discovering that her *Licenciatura* thesis was to study coastal birds she felt that her luck had eluded her. Birds were really not her thing, *'At that time I could just about make out a duck from a seagull'* she confessed.

In 1989, unenthusiastically, and armed just with a black-and-white field guide, she embarked on her studies. These studies were made all the more difficult as nobody in the town where she was operating, San Antonio Oeste in Argentina, knew about birds to answer her questions. In those days there was also no internet on which to rely for additional information, leaving her bereft of inspiration when she needed it most, when the doubts crept in.

She began to scrutinise the huge intertidal areas around San Antonio Bay, which covers 10 km of coastline with the low tide mark being anything up to 7 km distant from the upper shore, aided only by a pair of her father's old binoculars.

'For a long time the beaches appeared deserted, and any hope of finding any birds at all also deserted me until, one day, everything changed: thousands of shorebirds in the form of red knots, sanderlings and white-rumped sandpipers arrived.' At least now she had something to study, but she wasn't prepared

for the effect that the birds would have on her.

'Their great aerial figures were art in the sky, but discovering them in closer detail through my father's binoculars was quite a life changing experience. I watched them eat voraciously knowing that they had travelled from the Arctic, far to the north, to Tierra del Fuego to the south of San Antonio Bay where I was watching them. They were now on their way back north again on their way to their Arctic breeding grounds. This realisation awakened in me a unique sensation of admiration for those beings, so small, and yet, so powerful.'

Binoculars had opened up this new direction that took her to encounter so many of her tiny migratory friends in many countries along their flyway. Patricia was touched and captivated by the amazing lifestyle of the birds she studied and in the end became an ambassador for them.

'There is a great lesson to be had from this' she said, *'which I use every day. Binoculars are a rare and precious thing in our part of the world, but they are our secret weapon. If anyone ever says to me that they don't like birds I simply say to them that it is merely because they have never really looked at them. When it comes to enthusing people about birds a look through a pair of binoculars at their intricate beauty always changes things.'*

The work that Patricia began in 1989 resulted in the forming of the *Area Natural Protegida Bahía de San Antonio* (San Antonio Bay Protected Area) in 1993 and in 2018 the community will be celebrating those twenty-five years during the *Festival de Aves Playeras Bahía San Antonio* now in its ninth year.

A very significant name in the wader world is that of Clive

Minton, who was inspired by the humble sanderling and has gone on to become a towering figure in the world of waders and a pioneer of both wader ringing and wader trapping for scientific purposes. Clive told us that he started ringing waders when he was staying with a school friend in Bamburgh in Northumberland in August 1951. Whilst riding his bike on the beach one day he and his friend caught a small wader by hand (by throwing a coat over it). They were unable to identify it so they took it to the nearby Monks House Bird Observatory and presented it to the great artist and ornithologist Eric Ennion who ran the observatory. Eric informed the boys that it was a juvenile sanderling and this encounter led to great things in the wader ringing world.

Eric soon discovered that the two boys had a lot of expertise and experience in catching birds with clap nets. The three of them spent the rest of the boys' holiday building these nets together and successfully trying them out on the shore and on a small pool in a field near the observatory. In the early 1950s Clive and his Monk House friends formed a team that became the fourth largest ringing group in the UK with their annual totals published in *British Birds*. This was quite an achievement considering it was set in motion by the chance capture of a sanderling. It was also the start of wader ringing in the UK: they captured the first grey plover, ruff and common greenshank but that was just the beginning and another sanderling entered Clive's story.

'I subsequently spent most of my school and university holidays at Monks House. It was probably in August 1952 that we were clap-netting waders on a small ocean beach on Holy Island, about 10 miles north of Monks House. We caught the

first sanderling there. Great excitement – but even more so when only a month later the sanderling was reported in Turkey at the east end of the Black Sea. Totally unexpected location and therefore extremely exciting and stimulating.'

Clive points out that if you look at the sanderling recoveries map in the comprehensive BTO publication of recoveries of all species, about 10 years ago, you will see a little black dot showing where this bird was recovered and how unique such a movement really was.

'So I've always had a great liking for sanderling. It led me to meet Dr Ennion, who has had more influence on my life than anyone but my parents. It led to the start of wader ringing in Britain and it ultimately led me to meeting my future wife in 1957, at Monks House.'

Pat and Clive have been married now for 58 years and Clive tells me that they still have the original painting Eric Ennion gave to them as a wedding present in 1959 of a Common and Spotted Redshank together; quite some present. Sadly Monks House closed down in the early 1960s when Eric and his wife decided they were too elderly to run such a demanding operation.

Clive went on to be a guiding light in the wader ringing movement himself in the UK establishing the Wash Wader Ringing Group and inspiring others with his methods of capturing waders. He developed the canon netting process that was borrowed first from Peter Scott and then the Ministry of Agriculture and adapting it to suit waders. Chance took him, through work, to Australia and there he found a blank page upon which he could write himself into the annals of waderology history again and did so with energy and enthusiasm. So much of what we know about waders today can be attributed to Clive and the methods that he created, the organisations that he founded - such as the Victoria and Australian Wader Study Groups (VWSG & AWSG) - and the ideas that he has developed.

Richard Chandler has written a number of books about waders, the latest being the fascinating *Shorebirds in Action*. He is another who freely admits that waders are an obsession. His interest started during an academic research expedition to high Arctic Spitsbergen in the early 1970s, where he was involved in geotechnical engineering, not avian biology. There were no flights to the area then and so he made a long voyage on a 'fast' mail boat leaving Bergen, sailing north up the Norwegian coast, across the Barents Sea, past Bear Island, to the Svalbard archipelago. Richard realised he needed something to occupy his time and having treated himself to a pair of binoculars a few months earlier, the obvious solution was - bird watching!

'My list of birds seen during the expedition was quite short, particularly in Spitzbergen itself, but it included a few shorebird species: breeding grey phalaropes, a single, off-route red knot (and it was red, in full breeding plumage), and purple sandpipers, which confused me as they had darkish, not yellow legs, though the book I had with me implied that yellow legs were an important field mark. I later discovered that the field guide omitted to mention that their leg colour got darker in the breeding season!

A few months later, now with a real interest in shorebirds, a visit to the Isle of Sheppey in Kent, UK, again found me puzzling over shorebird identity - this time different species were involved, and they all looked confusingly similar. So similar that I was not only confused, but even challenged to put a name to them; I needed to know more!'

A year or two later he discovered that his local library subscribed to the journal *British Birds* (BB), where he found a recently published article that featured photos of shorebirds by the husband-and-wife team Brian and Sheila Bottomley (BB 1976, 69, 155). A follow-up letter in BB from Clive Minton (BB 69, 514) showed how much could be learnt from high quality photographic images. *'... and I was hooked, both by the shorebirds themselves, and now on photographing them too. And, more than forty years on, I am still at it, and still learning from watching and photographing shorebirds.'*

Mary Colwell is an award-winning TV, radio and internet producer. Mary has a particular interest in the natural world and recently published a book, *Curlew Moon*, about her involvement with the conservation of Eurasian Curlews in the British Isles. She was recently awarded the BTO Dilys Breese Medal for outstanding Communication in Science. This award was a result of the intense connection with the Eurasian curlew that she has developed.

In the spring of 2016 Mary was motivated to raise awareness about the challenges being faced by the declining Eurasian curlew population. To do so she decided to walk 500 miles across the British Isles from the west coast of Ireland to the east coast of England via Wales. As a result of that a 'Curlews in Crisis' workshop was held in Ireland and this resulted in the 'Curlew Task Force' being set up with the aim of encouraging protection of these birds in the subsequent breeding season.

In early 2017, a second workshop was held at WWT Slimbridge that resulted in the 'Southern Curlew Forum', which brings together many working on curlews and offers a platform for advice and information exchange. Following this she planned the Welsh Curlew Conference in early 2018 to highlight the plight of the curlew throughout Wales.

But why had curlews struck Mary in particular? Well actually she had been forced to ask herself the same question due to a bit of tongue-in-cheek ribbing from her youngest son when he threatened to take her to the wildlife equivalent of the Equal Opportunities Commission.

'Why just curlews? What about blackbirds or albatrosses, herons or pigeons?' he quizzed.

'Well, blackbirds don't need much help at the moment, and albatrosses are big and charismatic, so many people are noticing what is happening to them' she replied.

But his question was a good one and surprisingly hard to answer Mary admits, and it made her rake through her memory to try to find out why these birds in particular strike a chord.

'Twenty years ago, I clearly remember watching a lone curlew on a very cold and blustery beach in North Somerset. The wind was bitter, a typical January day that sucked away any warmth from my body. Being inside with tea and crumpets seemed a better option than wader-watching from an empty car park by the sea. But for some reason, I couldn't tear myself away. Despite my fingers and cheeks going numb, the solitary curlew was magnetic. It occupied that mysterious interface

between land and sea, the liminal, shifting boundary where we have no place. Despite the wind threatening to blow it off its thin, stilt-like legs, it seemed in control - almost Zen like. And then, suddenly, it took off. It launched itself into the air and let out its magical, piercing 'curlee' call that fired across the sand like an arrow. My soul was spirited to a place of yearning and joy, sorrow and beauty. As it disappeared over the horizon and it took a part of me with it. And so, when I discovered a few years ago how seriously curlews are declining, I felt I had no choice but to do something.'

Mary then went on to explain her fears for the species.

'Reversing the decline of the Eurasian curlew is a gargantuan task. They face many problems that can only be solved by nothing less than a major transformation of the way we farm food and how we use the land. If we don't rise to the challenge, they may well slip away very quickly, and the world will be impoverished. We will not just lose another species, we will lose a mysterious bird that has inspired so much creativity and joy. It will be a tragedy.'

David Turner lives in North Yorkshire and has been a long serving member of the IWSG Executive Committee, acting as Treasurer for the group, and has led the Humber Wader Ringing Group (HWRG) for the last fifteen years. However he has not always lived so close to the Humber. He started ringing in the mid-70's with the Banbury Ornithological Society, about as far from the coast as you can get in the UK and a long way from the Humber. There he learned a great deal and with a friend he decided it would be good experience to go on a ringing course at Spurn Bird Observatory. David remembers:

'While, even then, it was well known as a migration site, it was my first real experience of the Humber Estuary. I recall vividly the large numbers of waders, and the feeling that I was in a really 'wild' place. It all lingered in my mind, but I didn't, couldn't at that time, do anything more about it. But, it left an image and lots and lots of questions; where do the waders come from? Where are they going? Why do they stay? What are they eating?

The Humber estuary and its waders certainly had a lasting effect on me, I remember thinking, wow! What a wild place! I couldn't (until very recently) think of anywhere so wild and yet so close to 'civilisation'. Within twenty five miles you could go from being in an urban environment to being in the wild; and it was really wild in the 1970's.'

But what really got to David were those unanswered questions about the waders. He was impressed by the logistics and scale of these movements, the distances they travel from their breeding grounds in the far north, Greenland or northern Scandinavia, to stop over to feed up for a while in the Humber and move on, or stay for the winter.

'By the time the birds reached the Humber they had already travelled about 1,750 miles! If they then move on to winter in Africa, that adds another 2,500 miles, about the distance from the UK to Beijing and then they had to fly all the way back again to breed!'

Following some time taken away from ringing because of growing commitments to family and work, in the early 1990's David moved to North Yorkshire and returned to ringing. Fortuitously his ringing trainer was involved in the Spurn

Ringing Courses.

Independently from his trainer, through a ringing course in 1994 where he hoped to re-gain his 'C' permit, he re-engaged with wild Spurn, and the Humber Estuary. He once again experienced the feeling of being in a truly wild place.

'Mud, sand and hundreds, no, thousands, of waders... red knots, dunlins, redshanks, godwits, oystercatchers and curlews. All of the feelings and questions came flooding back to me, and, more importantly, I started to think about what I could do to help preserve all that was good for them on the Humber estuary.'

In addition to David's involvement with the Humber he is now studying waders, particularly Eurasian curlew, breeding on the North York Moors as well as undertaking a number of other bird ringing & surveying projects, but he concludes:

'There's nothing that quite compares to the 'wild' habitats where the waders breed, and similarly, generally, where they either stage or over-winter before returning to breed again.'

In the north-west of England lies the Dee Estuary, a magnet for visiting waders that gather in roosts of many thousands at high tide around the coast at West Kirby. This is a time when the birds are very vulnerable to disturbance, just when they need to be resting. Fortunately for them the Dee Estuary Voluntary Wardens (DEVW) monitor these high tide roosts during the winter and engage with the public to educate them about the birds' needs or simply show the wonderful spectacle to passers-by. The DEVW, created in 1986, is a collaboration between the Local Authority (Wirral Borough Council), English Nature (as Natural England was then known) and local birders to protect the wading flocks from disturbance.

Someone who has been a part of the DEVW for nearly all that period, and is now the long standing Chair of the DEVW committee is Karen Leeming, and she has explained how she came to be so involved in protecting waders.

'It was almost 30 years ago on a grey, windy day with a really high tide whipping the edges of the dunes at West Kirby that I fell in love with waders. I hadn't been birding very long but I'd heard the beach was one of the best places to see waders in winter. So, I'd made my way along the boardwalk and was just about to climb a dune when two winter-clad women appeared from nowhere and stopped me. 'You can't go over there, you'll disturb them' – I wasn't quite sure what they meant but they showed me badges and assured me that they were there to stop people disturbing the wader flock. I was encouraged to get down on my hands and knees and crawl to the top of the dune very quietly and I would see something amazing. They were right. Crammed into the base of the dunes and stretching all along the beach were tens of thousands of knot and dunlin chipping and burbling away and I was transfixed by the numbers and the noise – an unexpected coup de foudre.'

Not long after this introduction Karen too became one of those winter-clad wardens and was paired with two 'old school' birders, Carl and Chris who, over the next couple of years taught Karen both identification and counting skills, eventually announcing that she was ready to become a Wetland Bird Survey (WeBS) counter.

'I never expected my unintended love affair with waders

to have shaped my life in the way that it has. I'm still a WeBS counter, I'm still with the DEVW, I volunteer with the RSPB at the Burton Mere Wetlands reserve, and I lead the committee for the Wirral Wader Festival, which was initiated in 2015, the first of its type in the UK, on those very same beaches where my love affair began.'

Waders are endearing and fascinating. Once they have your attention, they do not easily relent. There is always something more to learn, which is equally, and often more, intriguing than that which you already know. On a more superficial level they are entrancing with their agility and elegant beauty. As a result, waders have spawned many groups of enthusiasts around the world, perhaps more so than any other group of birds.

With the possible exception of raptors, there are few specialist celebrations of bird families to be found around the world. However, there are a number of wader and shorebird festivals, some of which have been running annually for many years. On the north-west coast of North America in Canada and the USA there are several shorebird festivals; the Copper Delta Shorebird Festival (28 years), the Kachemak Bay Shorebird Festival (26 years), the Tofino Shorebird Festival (21 years) with yet another at Gray's Harbour (23 years) and perhaps the grand-daddy of them all the Oregon Shorebird Festival (32 years).

On the east coast of North America there is the world famous Horsehoe Crab and Shorebird Festival in Delaware Bay (15 years) and the Jamaica Bay Shorebird Festival in New York (13 years).

South America has also joined in the celebrations with

festivals for *Aves Playeras*, as waders are widely known, in Rio Gallegos and San Antonio Bay in Argentina and, the new kid on the block, Puerto Rico where they held their first in 2017. In Australia the Adelaide Shorebird Festival had the slogan 'Inspiring South Australia', very apt.

It was looking at these events that Elis and I decided that we should attend a wader festival in the UK. To our dismay we found there were none. This further inspired us to approach the DEVW to set up the UK's first ever wader festival in 2015 on the Wirral in north-west England, collaborating with the RSPB, the Cheshire Wildlife Trust and Wirral Council; there have been festivals there ever since. In addition, Wader Quest has been invlved in other festivals such as the Wash Wader Festival at Titchwell RSPB reserve in Norfolk in conjunction with the RSPB, the South Walney Island Wader Festival with the Cumbria Wildlife Trust, and the Severn Wader Festival held at Slimbridge WWT in Gloucestershire.

Why should it be that waders attract this attention from individuals and groups? Is there a particular type of person that becomes imbued by the sense of collectiveness of waders? It was once suggested to me that specialist ornithological enthusiasts admire the birds they do because they match their own character. The person who suggested this then went on to say that wader enthusiasts like to flock together, like the waders themselves, because they are naturally gregarious. To add weight to his theory the person expressed the opinion that raptor enthusiasts are loners, preferring not to work in groups, much as raptors themselves are apt to be, and gull aficionados are noisy!

Chapter Three

Inspiring art, music and literature

'The lapwing of course, needs no introduction. If it were not for its being so common it would assuredly be thought of more highly than it is.'

Birds of Britain (1962) - Kenneth Richmond (1910- 1990)

Ever since we humans ceased to look at the world around us simply as a source of food and started appreciating other forms of life as objects of beauty, waders have been inspiring us with their grace and beauty, as well as their amazing diversity and talents. From the moment the stone-age equivalent of Banksy set about defacing the inside of his or her living quarters by depicting the animals and birds with which people shared their environment, we have been moved to record our wonderful world in one way or another.

These early artworks have been followed by works in many media through the millennia. The northern lapwing was, for example, commonly depicted in the Egyptian paintings and reliefs decorating palaces and temples from about 3,000 BC onwards. The Egyptians often illustrated wildlife along the Nile and in the adjacent marshes. At that time, the lapwing was apparently a popular children's pet and its image was commonly painted with the bird's wings pinioned to prevent them from flying.

The lapwing, unmistakeable with its crest, can also be found in Egyptian hieroglyphs and is said to have represented the people of Lower Egypt. This may have been due to it being an obvious bird that wintered in good numbers in the Delta. From the 18th Dynasty (1549 BC to 1292 BC), and thereafter, the hieroglyph of a lapwing came to mean 'a group of people' and a lapwing with raised human arms, as though held in prayer, meant 'a group of people giving praise'.

More traditional art, in the form of painting and drawing on more conventional media was however slow to pick up on the possibilities of waders. This may reflect a lack of interest or respect for the natural world as a whole at that time. Artists are, by their very nature, keen observers so they are unlikely to have missed them entirely. I think it fair to say that, beyond those with an actual interest in zoology, waders and everything else slipped under the radar as far as the old masters are concerned although John Turner (1775 - 1851) did produce some bird artworks for the *Ornithological Collection* at Farnley Hall with twenty different bird paintings. Tellingly of these twenty (which included one wader, a woodcock), four of them were shown as corpses perhaps reflecting the relationship we had with nature in those days.

If you look at old landscape paintings depicting an estuary or seascape, a genre in which Turner excelled, the scene will be replete with portrayals of human activities, such as fisher folk going about their business, as well as occasionally a bit of conflict between stately ships with billowing sails, or the odd perilous storm catching sailing boats and ships unaware. What you will not see, however, are waders. It almost appears that the estuaries were devoid of waders in those days, which surely cannot be the case. More general scenes sometimes contain the odd childlike bird in flight, some distance away, characterised by a shallow V or an L-shaped form supposed to represent a duck of some sort. The only pictures that illustrated waders in any recognisable form were those of dead birds having been hunted for the pot. An example of this is Peter Paul Rubens' (1577 – 1640) '*Diana Returning from the Hunt*' (1615) where a generic wader species, possibly a curlew, is slung under Diana's arm along with a variety of other unfortunate fowl. Another is Salomon van Ruysdel's (1600 – 1670) '*A Still Life With A Cockerel, Two Lapwings, A Duck And Other Birds, All On A Stone Ledge*' (1660). It strikes my obtuse mind that it is something of an irony that a painting can be referred to as still life when all the subjects within it are actually still as a result of being *devoid* of life. There are few exceptions to this restricted depiction of wildlife simply as food.

Rubens and Jan Brueghel the Elder (1568 – 1625) jointly produced a number of paintings in which Rubens painted the human figures and Brueghel the animals and birds. These are done in such a way that most are instantly recognisable. Some of these paintings depicted life in paradise, with a strange combination of creatures living in incongruous harmony. In these Brueghel fashioned lapwings and snipe as part of the menagerie.

A few artists of sea and coast have placed intriguing and tantalising shapes on the sand of their beach and estuary scenes but have not made them specifically identifiable as waders; gulls being more likely. One work however, called *'Waft of Mist'* (1820) by Caspar David Friedrich (1774 - 1840), has captured, with a clear understanding and feeling for the birds' characteristic flight, the moment when a flock of lapwings is descending to a field. But none of the great landscape artists, as far as I can see, paid any heed to the evocative swirling masses of waders that there must have been on those estuaries of yore.

Within the ranks of artistic naturalists there has been a great change in how birds have been depicted over the last couple of centuries. Images by pioneers such as John James Audubon (1785 - 1851) and John Gould (1804 - 1881) are, to our modern eyes, rather bizarre with birds posed in such a way that in some cases they defy biology. To be fair however, it should be remembered that many of these drawings and paintings were made with nothing more than a skin from which to work, these gentlemen never having laid eyes on the birds alive. More recently, however, many more people have taken to harnessing their artistic talents to depict the beauty of waders in the form of paintings and sculptures, some of which are so incredibly life-like that you expect them to move, call or blink at any moment. The works of the early pioneers, and the upper echelons of modern bird artists, do though have one thing in common: if you wish to be the proud owner of an original, you will need a sizeable disposable income.

Western music, within the limits of my knowledge and

experience, has also paid scant attention to waders although names of groups are to be found bearing wader names such as The Shorebirds, The Sandpipers, Plover, Lapwings, Whimbrel and Curlew. There is though a traditional jig called *The Curlew* with many versions featuring, in the main, the fiddle.

I have been unable to track down actual lyrical content, at least in English, with the exception of my own ditty about the spoon-billed sandpiper (lyrics in Appendix II). There have, nevertheless, been songs written in other tongues that do include waders. One such in Hawai'i concerns the wandering tattler which is called ''*Ulili E'* and a rather pleasing rendition of it is sung by Israel Kamakawiwo'ole (1959 – 1997) in the local Hawaiian language '*Ōlelo Hawai'i*. The song alludes to the habitat and character of the species and conjures mental images of the tattler running along peaceful and calm beaches emitting a soft and sweet call. The tattler keeps watch over the beaches, the story teller informs us, and he or she says to the tattler, '*You grace our land, where the sea is always calm'*. Israel's soft voice, coupled with the lyrical language and the pleasant melody, certainly evoke a utopian picture of a peaceful tropical beach, with a gentle sea lapping quietly on the shore and a small bird quietly watching over it.

Another melodic and accomplished song is in Dutch, composed by Dutch-Frisian musician Syb van der Ploeg and, entitled *De koning van de weide* (King of the Meadows). This was written to celebrate the black-tailed godwit when it was voted Dutch National Bird in November 2015.

In classical music the situation doesn't seem to be significantly better. However French composer Olivier Messiaen (1908 – 1992) in his *Catalogue D'oiseaux* Book 7 (1956-58) created *Le Courlis cendré* (Eurasian curlew) a rather unusual piano piece which includes some distinct passages redolent with the curlew's calls; in particular the rising warbles for which the bird is perhaps best known. In addition the Finn Einojuhani Rautavaara (1928 – 2016) created a piece of music using real Arctic bird song in the background as part of the piece called *Cantus Arcticus* (1972). Benjamin Britten (1913-1976) also wrote an operatic piece called *Curlew River*, based on a Japanese tale, setting his piece in East Anglia and the fens.

Although not strictly music, some may remember a vinyl recording called *'Big Jake calls the Waders'* in which Jake Ward imitated wader calls. These imitations were tweaked electronically, and designed to be an educational aid to birdwatchers. Sadly I never possessed a copy.

In the written word waders have fared rather better, they get a mention from time to time in plays, poetry and prose. They are often used to inspire imagery of landscapes, desolate places and at other times to illustrate a human trait of some kind.

Among the waders most often thus characterised are the Eurasian curlew and the northern lapwing, probably because they were once both very common, highly visible and distinctly audible to anyone who was lucky enough to live near them.

It is the curlew's call that is alluded to most often, wild and eerily haunting, melancholy and yet beautiful. Indeed, it seems to be its call that has drawn attention to this species rather than its rather drab looks, despite that amazing bill.

Soothed by the murmurs of the sea-beat shore,
His dun-gray plumage floating to the gale,

The curlew blends his melancholy wail,
With those hoarse sounds the rushing waters pour.

(Helen Maria Williams: 1762-1827)

You won't find many articles written about the curlew that don't contain the word evocative. The curlew's call is very distinctive, once heard it is never forgotten and is often used to describe desolate places and melancholy in poems old and new. Due to the fall in curlew numbers it could now be indicative of the bird's own sorrow at its looming demise, rather like an old man wailing whilst awaiting the uninvited grim reaper. It would be a tragedy indeed if the characteristic call of this bird, so haunting and suggestive of moorland and open, unpeopled landscapes, were to be lost to us forever. In a case of be-careful-what-you-wish-for it seems that W. B. Yeats (1865-1939) may yet get the wish he expressed in his poem *O CURLEW, cry no more in the air* where the rising lament of the curlew serves as a reminder of a lost love in a short, but surprisingly sensual, piece.

O, CURLEW, cry no more in the air,
Or only to the water in the West;
Because your crying brings to my mind
Passion-dimmed eyes and long heavy hair
That was shaken out over my breast:
There is enough evil in the crying of wind.

To me there is something soothing and relaxing about the rippling riff of the curlew's call, a sound that fills me with a kind of calmness when I hear it. It never fails to put a smile on my face, but Sir Walter Scott (1771–1832) heard no beauty the call at all it would appear:

Wild as the scream of the curlew,
From rock to rock the signal flew.

The great bard himself, William Shakespeare (1564 – 1616), was inspired in his writings to link two of the northern lapwing's traits to those of his characters. One of these characteristics that appears in his works, and one that the lapwing shares with most other waders, is that the chicks are of a precocial nature; which is to say that they are in an advanced state of maturity, being able to feed and walk independently, almost immediately upon hatching. In *Hamlet*, Horatio says of Osrick, to infer that he was quick off the mark, perhaps a little too quick, and rather cocky and over sure of his abilities;

'This lapwing runs away with shell on his head.'

Another lapwing trait obliquely alluded to by Shakespeare in *Comedy of Errors* was the commonly held perception of the bird being deceitful in nature.

'Far from her nest the lapwing cries away.'

Shakespeare was not alone, nor the first, to express this poor opinion of the lapwing however. Before him Geoffrey Chaucer (1343 – 1400) referred to it as *'false lapwynge, ful of treacherye'*. John Gower (1330 – 1408) called them *'The bird falsest of all'* and William Caxton (c1422 – c1491) calls them *'foul and villainous'*, which all seems a bit harsh to me as in my opinion this bird is both clever and noble in its defence of its nest and young. A discussion on this subject is dealt with later. It was though, one supposes, a very common and familiar bird in those days and an obvious subject for writers and poets, however misguided they may have been.

Emily Brontë (1818 – 1848) referred to the lapwing in *Wuthering Heights*, when Cathy was identifying feathers that had come from a pillow she had torn asunder with her teeth in a fit of pique:

'... and this – I should know it among a thousand – it's a lapwing's. Bonny bird; wheeling over our head in the middle of the moor.'

As Brönte had noted lapwings are also well known for their exaggerated gyrations during the breeding season when it is not only their call that is easily recognisable. The sound of their wings, which visually resemble a winnowing fan, from which they gain the scientific name of *Vanellus*, scything through the air is also very distinctive.

> *Here did I roam while veering overhead*
> *The Pewet whirred in many whewing wings*
> *& 'chewsit' screamed & clapped her flapping wings*
> (John Clare 1793 – 1864)

John Clare also wrote *To The Snipe* which describes the chosen, hidden habitat of the snipe, distancing itself from the haunts of humanity,

> *Lover of swamps*
> *The quagmire overgrown*
> *With hassock-tufts of sedge — where fear encamps*
> *Around thy home alone...*

and for good reason...

> *Yet instinct knows*
> *Not safety's bounds:—to shun*
> *The firmer ground where skulking fowler goes*
> *With searching dogs and gun.*

A wader that was presumably not as widely encountered as the previous species, due to its lifestyle being rather more restricted to coastal districts, was the red knot. Nevertheless, this bird got a mention, as did many others, in Drayton's Poly-Olbion with an allusion to the origins of its name which are supposed to be in relation to King Canute's preference for its flesh;

> *The knot, that called was Canutus' bird of old.*
> *Of that great king of Danes, his name that still doth hold.*
> *His appetite to please, that far and near was sought.*
> *For him, as some have said, from Denmark hither brought.*

(Michael Drayton 1563-1631)

There are also many talented modern day writers and poets who have been inspired by waders. However it is not always the positive and wonderful that has inspired them. The Eurasian curlew population in the British Isles is, as alluded to earlier, in steep decline and this had prompted a movement of concerned people and organisations to attempt to halt, or better still reverse, this trend. As part of this campaign, creative writer and poet Karen Lloyd devised and edited an anthology of writings about the curlew, *Curlew Calling* (2017), even setting-up her own publishing company, Numenius Press in homage of the curlews (*Numenius* being the generic name for all curlews and whimbrels). In an excerpt from that book, within a poem by Lucy Grove entitled *A Shropshire Curlew*, the calamitous decline of the curlew is encapsulated in three simple lines;

> *'Grandad knew of dozens,*
> *Father a few,*
> *My son will not know you here –'*

What is particularly remarkable about this poem is that it was Lucy's first attempt and she was inspired to write it by her concern for the curlew that had declined dramatically in her local area.

She was shocked at the declines that curlews were facing

and, she confesses, equally shocked at her own lack of knowledge, as an ecologist, about this. It created a link in her mind between the silent loss of curlews on the farm in Shropshire, and this large scale decline that the species is suffering. Thinking back she realised that she had made the assumption that the curlews had just chosen to breed somewhere else, not that they were in serious trouble, perhaps summing up why this has been allowed to happen on such a large scale almost unnoticed.

As a scientist she felt the project was a bit 'arty' and not for her, however, one night, unable to sleep, she wrote the poem, in its near final form, in those night-time hours.

Lucy herself explained.

'That I wrote it, that it was accepted and published, liked by others, and even liked by me (I'm very self-deprecating!) was astonishing! [It is] a testament to the power of this bird I believe.'

The passage that is included here is, she says, *'the most powerful part ... it is loss, a statement of fact, a warning, and a cry for help...'*

There have been, quite remarkably some works of fiction written about waders. Perhaps the best known of these is the *Last of the Curlews* written by Fred Bodsworth (1918-2012). It is a tragic tale about the last two remaining Eskimo curlews. It creates a fictional migration of a lonely bird which encounters, against all the odds, due to the annihilated population, a mate. As they travel north to a place where they might breed the female is shot dead and that is the death knell of the species. It is powerful and moving.

Another story is a much more positive tale of birds

overcoming adversity caused by various forms of human activity, and nature, by Kenneth Allsop (1920-1973), *Adventure Lit Their Stars.* The book covers the colonisation of Great Britain by the little ringed plover. It is an adjective strewn book with florid descriptions of scenery and settings which covers much of the wildlife in the environment in which the little ringed plovers chose to nest. It weaves stories around the birds, one female in particular, and the wildlife around culminating in a dramatic ending where the nest of the plovers is saved by the actions of a man (recovering from a debilitating illness) and two boys (themselves reformed egg collectors) from the clutches of a dastardly and determined egg collector.

An investigative book, *Orison for a Curlew* by Horatio Clare, takes a journey around some of the last known locations where the probably now extinct slender-billed curlew was seen. It looks at why this legendary bird has disappeared and encounters some of the last people to see them. From my point of view as one who actually had the chance to go and see one, but failed miserably to do so, it encapsulates my frustration as vicariously I visit the last known haunts of this mysterious bird that lived among us, but does so no more.

Lastly of course, I feel compelled to mention our own offering, *Eury the Spoon-billed Sandpiper.* We wrote this with a view to enlightening children between the ages of six and eleven as to the trials and tribulations of a long distance migrant bird in the modern world. The ultimate plan is to provide copies to schools in those countries along the spoon-billed sandpiper's migration route, where a greater understanding of the bird's problems would aid its preservation and chances of survival. The story follows Eury from inside his egg until he takes a mate

Chapter Four

Inspiring myths and legends

'From the very earliest of times birds have been the nucleus round which ignorance and imagination have thrown many a halo of legendary narrative.'

Curiosities of Bird Life (1897) - Charles Dixon (1858 - 1926)

Waders for many years remained something of an enigma. But myths and legends are to be found throughout the course of human history due to the human propensity for intrigue and mystery and a need to explain the unexplainable. Some of these are probably based on some kind of fact, others are pure fantasy.

The Egyptian plover for example, until quite recently, was more widely known as the crocodile bird and probably still is in some circles. It was the Greek historian Herodotus in the 5th century BC who first suggested a link between the two creatures. It came about through a belief that the birds spent at least some of their time gleaning bits and pieces from the teeth of crocodiles as they lay basking with their great mouths gaping wide. There is however, up to now, no evidence whatsoever that this peculiar behaviour takes place; except for a few very well manipulated photographic fakes on the internet, apocryphal tales and hearsay. It is entirely possible, indeed likely, that these birds would be seen feeding around crocodiles loafing on the sand and possibly even running along their backs. They would be able to pick prey from the skin of the animals with little fear of being caught, however, knowing that crocodiles do catch birds at the water's edge it seems extremely improbable that if a bird were to enter a crocodile's mouth the reptile would be able to resist the temptation to eat it or that it wouldn't trigger a reflex action to snap the jaws shut.

Étienne Geoffroy Saint-Hilaire (1772–1844) suggested that the *Pluvier à collier interompu* - Kentish plover - is Herodotus' crocodile bird and Dr Andrew Leith Adams (1827–1882), suggested the spur-winged lapwing. Leigh Adams further adds that the spurs on the joint of the wing of this bird could be used to remind the crocodile of the bird's presence. Should the crocodile be careless enough to close its mouth with the lapwing inside, the bird could prod it on the sensitive inner surface of the mouth with these sharp weapons. He noted that this action would invariably refresh the memory of the sleepy crocodile as to its 'faithful dentists' presence causing it to open its mouth and allow the bird's escape; *'to whom one hopes he expresses profound regret'* Leith Adams added.

There is one particularly interesting first-hand account that appears to corroborate Leith Adams' assertion that it was the spur-winged lapwing which was the crocodile bird. This account appeared in the correspondence section of *Ibis* (1893, pp. 275-277). It was from a Mr J. M. Cook. In his letter he said that he and his brother-in-law had a pit dug in the sand of a large bank on the Nile in order that they could watch the crocodiles and their attendant spur-winged lapwing crocodile birds. The following morning at dawn they entered the pit and said that they watched the crocodiles haul themselves out of the water onto the bank. Cook then states that the crocodile birds approached the crocodiles which opened their mouths, the bird hopped in and the crocodile promptly shut its jaws! A few minutes later the croc released the bird which hopped out and ran to the water's edge. He was unable to see whether the bird drank or vomited at this stage but the bird immediately returned to the crocodile to repeat the whole process.

Cook then goes on to say that they watched this event occur three times whereupon they shot the birds concerned... charming! It sounds almost convincing but frankly I lost faith when he stated the crocodile closed its mouth with the bird inside.

Spur-winged lapwing is also said to feature in an Islamic legend in which Allah asked all living things, both great and small, to attend a feast. All came except the spur-winged lapwing. Allah rebuked the lapwing. The lapwing claimed that he had fallen asleep and forgot. Allah, who knows all things, knew he had lied and answered *'From this day forward thou shalt know no sleep.'* Whereupon he caused two spurs to grow on the points of the bird's shoulders so that he would suffer great pain if he tried to sleep by putting his head under his wing in typical bird fashion.

The northern lapwing, a very familiar bird in Europe and the UK's most common wader, does not carry such spurs. With a bird as familiar as this is, or perhaps was in more superstitious times, it is inevitably going to have many myths surrounding it.

The collective noun for northern lapwings is, to my immense displeasure, a deceit. What foul calumny is this? Why should it be that such a noble and attractive bird in so many ways has attracted such a negative collective noun?

It is widely written, and supposed, that this deceit lay in the fact that northern lapwings perform a broken wing display when you approach their nest, but personally I have never seen lapwings engage in such shenanigans. John Wolley in his *Ootheca Wolleyana* (1864) wrote of this; *'I never myself saw the old bird feign lameness, and should fancy it only does so when it has young.'* Now this does make sense. The further advanced the development of the offspring is, the greater the effort that has been put into rearing them. Once hatched parent birds are less likely to lay a second clutch than if the first clutch of eggs is lost. Whilst this distraction display is definitely common in many *Charadrius* plovers, it is not common among lapwings. I do not contend that it never happens, for there are plenty who have written that it does, it's just that it doesn't seem to be a common lapwing trait so I asked myself, is it really this that has led to its insulting collective noun?

One alternative to this explanation might be that the idea has come from the disturbed nesting bird strategically placing itself in a position diametrically opposed to an intruder with relation to the nest position, whilst making scandalous demonstrations; but then what bird doesn't do this? This display is not peculiar to the lapwing. You can also find a further putative explanation along this same theme, in a literary book with the incredible title *'A glossary; or, a collection, of words, phrases, names and allusions to custom, proverbs &c. which have been thought to require illustration in the works of English authors particularly Shakespeare and his contemporaries.'* (1822) by Robert Nares. In it Nares suggests that the closer one gets to a northern lapwing's nest, the less scandalous and demonstrative it becomes. The idea presumably is that the bird is using subterfuge to make you think you are getting further from its nest. Again, in my experience, the nearer one approaches a lapwing's nest the louder and more insistent they become. However this theory is supported by the lines in John Clare's poem *Birds In Alarm.*

> *The pewit hollos 'chewrit' as she flies*
> *And flops about the shepherd where he lies;*
> *But when her nest is found she stops her song*
> *And cocks [her] coppled crown and runs along.*

There is yet another proposed explanation suggesting that it is in fact a misinterpretation of a foreign word. In England the northern lapwing is, or was, commonly known as a peewit, after its call. In Dutch it is *kievit* for the same reason and in some regions the French have a similar name, they call it '18' *dix -huit* (pronounced more or less desweet). Some claim that the idea of deceit came from this word being used in days of old. It is suggested that during the melding of French and English after 1066, the two meanings got mixed up. Try to imagine if you will a Norman Lord astride his horse, spotting a flock of lapwings, whipping out his ancient 10 x 30s and shouting *'Dix-huit! Dix-huit!'* caught up in the moment of excitement with adding lapwing to his English list, and the Anglo Saxon surfs getting entirely the wrong idea. Wishing to please their master, and no doubt spare their lives, having got the wrong end of the stick they started referring to the 'flock of *hleapewince*', as they might have previously been calling them, *hleapwince* being the old English name for the lapwing, as a 'deceit of *hleapewince*' instead.

Charming though this story is, albeit a little fanciful, it would not explain why the ancient Greeks had a mistrust of the northern lapwing and considered it deceitful, after all France and the French and even the Men from the North (Normans) with their wonderful language did not exist in those days.

In Ancient Greece, it is interesting to note that the name for lapwing was *polyplagktos* which means, 'luring on deceitfully'. The ancient Greeks also had an expression for cunning beggars describing them as '*more beseechful than a lapwing*'. So it is clear that this idea goes back a long way.

Myths and legends have bestowed human traits on many of the creatures that we have encountered over the years of our cultural evolution, some to the distinct detriment of the species concerned. It would appear that the idea of the lapwing being deceitful could even stem from the king of the Greek gods himself, Zeus. Zeus was supposed to have the ability to change his appearance at will and used this gift to seduce many women. Among these ladies that were thus deceived was Lamia, the beautiful Queen of Libya, whom he seduced when he transformed himself into a lapwing. The wife of Zeus, Hera (apparently the only person or thing of which Zeus was fearful) was incensed by this treachery and stole Lamia's children. This foul deed turned Lamia into a monster that, seeking revenge, then stole other people's children devouring them and sucking their blood. Charming lot those Greek gods and mythical creatures, especially as Hera was not only Zeus' wife but also his sister; not really the sort of thing with which our noble lapwings ought to be associated. But maybe there's a clue here about where the deceitful bit came from after all. Was it that cad, the philandering Zeus, which has given such a bad name to the lapwing?

Whatever the reason for the association of northern lapwings with deceitful ways, it is clear that centuries of time are not enough to exonerate oneself; once you have a reputation it is hard to shift it. It would be very agreeable if we could try to find a better collective noun for our beloved northern lapwing, but in the meantime you can hear the frustrated lapwing's cry to this day as they pass over the spring meadows, dipping and swerving, mad with indignity *'It wasn't me! It wasn't me!'* Go on, go out and listen, if you can still find one.

According to Cornelius Agrippa a 16th century philosopher the lapwing was afforded royal status due to it having a crown upon its head. It is unclear from whence this idea came but some suggest it may be that he was referring, in some oblique way, to the mention of the bird in the *Bible* (Leviticus XI: 19). This is the passage where the animals that were to be considered unclean, and therefore unfit for human consumption, were being announced by Moses. In that motley crew of unclean flesh was the lapwing. The reason given for its inclusion, it is supposed, is that it ate insects from cow dung. However in another version of the same biblical text, the same bird is referred to as the hoopoe which is more likely to have been seen in those areas, almost certainly doing just that, and whose crest much more resembles a crown than that of the lapwing. A Roman poet by the name of Ovid suggested that the hoopoe was a sacred bird as it carried a crown upon its head and that the lapwing was deceitful in that it impersonated the sacred hoopoe by sporting a crown in the form of a crest. These are not the only examples where these two birds have been associated, or even substituted, one for the other. In the *Qur'an* the lapwing has been cited as being the repository of Solomon's secrets and the most intelligent of the flock of prophetic birds that attended him, however some versions of the same text also refer in this context to the hoopoe.

There are other ancient tales where hoopoes and lapwings are interchangeable in various versions of myths such as the story of the wicked Tereus who raped his sister-in-law, Philomela, and then cut out her tongue to silence her before they, together with his wife Procne, were all turned into birds. In Ovid's version Tereus became a hoopoe but in later versions by John Dryden (1631-1700) and Gower, the bird in question is a lapwing.

However, the hoopoe is not the only candidate for confusion with lapwings among these ancient legends. Another example of a different species appearing in alternative versions of the same legend, in the same role as the lapwing occurs, once more in Ancient Greece. Daedalus threw poor Talos, his nephew, from the Acropolis wall. This was because Talos was too good at his job, hence threatening Daedalus' status as the best architect and craftsman in the world. The story goes that Talos was saved during his fall by the Goddess Athena who caught him and, according to some interpretations, turned him into a lapwing. Others though believe the bird concerned was a partridge, which actually much better fits the myth in that the bird resulting from this transmogrification nested on the ground, was afraid of heights and never flew high as a result. (This is further endorsed by a synonym of Talos = Perdix which is now used as the generic name for partridges).

The tale of the Easter Bunny, which refers to a rabbit that is the bringer of eggs, also has a connection to the great, cultural, avian icon the northern lapwing. The Easter Bunny story has its roots in pagan times because lapwings often laid their eggs in the forms made by European hares, finding them a convenient place to nest. The people who found these eggs in the form, unencumbered by knowledge of biology, zoology or ornithology, believed they had been placed there by the hare. This belief came about because of the pagan goddess Eostre. (It is no coincidence that the name resembles Easter.) It is said that Eostre found an injured bird, some versions specifically name the lapwing, one winter. To save its life, for some reason, she deemed it necessary to turn it into a hare. However the transformation was not complete and the hare was still able to lay eggs, which it did every spring in honour of Eostre. As if this wasn't enough the hare was said to decorate the eggs to make them special. But how or why did the hare become a bunny?

Hares have a strong connection to old pagan culture as symbols of fertility and therefore a little bit *risqué*. As a result they were an anathema to the staunchly Christian sensitivities which prevailed after the pagan times in Europe. Accordingly the hare morphed into the innocuous rabbit and the result is your egg producing Easter Bunny. What the Christians failed to grasp, rather ironically, is that rabbits breed like... well... rabbits.

There can exist few more natural celebrations of fertility than a buck rabbit.

So next time you bite the head off a chocolate Easter Bunny, stop and think of the lapwings fluting and pirouetting insanely across the springtime meadows as they are irretrievably linked to your chocolate treat today.

In the South of Scotland the lapwing was also looked upon with a good deal of suspicion especially along the border with England. A group of Scottish Presbyterians, known as the Covenanters, were much persecuted during the reign of King Charles II and as they crept about the land trying to evade their persecutors they were sometimes given away by the scolding attentions of the lapwings.

Conversely, a rather more positive result of the lapwing's attentions was displayed when an ancient Lincolnshire family, the Tyrwhitts, placed three lapwings on their coat of arms. This was because one of the family founders was injured during a skirmish and was discovered by his followers because they had been directed to his location by the cries of the vexed lapwings hovering in the vicinity. As an aside here, rare though this incorporation of waders in a coat of arms is, it is not unique. The town of Ashburton in New Zealand has two white-headed stilts incorporated in its coat of arms. (See also page 74.)

It is pleasing here to inject another note of positivity with an opinion of the northern lapwing much more in line with my own. It comes from one William Groundwater in his book *The Birds and Mammals of Orkney* (1974). In it he refers to the lapwing's spring calls as having a '*haunting quality of its own*' that puts one in mind of the coming season, of warming days and the promise of the summer to follow. He describes too its good character, which, let's face it, makes a pleasant change. He says it has *'a quiet dignity, stateliness and firm composure, its stance erect and dignified'.* He goes on to say that *'it broods with an inward calm stability, quiet and purposeful yet without a trace of servile or crouching timidity. It is watchful, anxious and brave, not easily flustered or startled but ready to defend its territory with vigour and courage against all interlopers, bird or beast'.* I find myself in complete agreement, that is the lapwing that I recognise and admire.

Another regional legend to have come to light during recent reading of old poetry and literature, comes from the North Riding of Yorkshire. There persisted a belief that once upon a time the woodpigeon laid its eggs on the ground, and that the lapwing made its nest in trees. For some inexplicable and untold reason they decided to swap nesting locations. The result was that now the lapwing expresses its feeling of having got the worst of the deal by calling;

Peewit, peewit !
I coup'd my nest and I rue it.'

The pigeon on the other hand is delighted with the outcome leaving her nest out of reach of mischievous children;

'Coo, coo, come now,
Little lad,
With thy gad,
Come not thou.'

(Anon.)

Other lapwing species from further afield have also attracted the attentions of the mythmakers. In India the red-wattled lapwings were widely believed to incubate their eggs by placing their backs over them with their legs pointing skywards. It was believed that the legs are held up in this fashion to prevent the sky from falling down on the eggs. This myth was so persistent that there is even a ten cent stamp depicting a lapwing on its back. However, one can occasionally see a red-wattled lapwing adopting this position in order to ward off an attacking bird to protect its eggs. The defending lapwing attacks an aerial intruder with its sharp claws and takes up this position in order to effectively aim its well-armed, long toes at the enemy, usually concentrating its attack on the head of the adversary.

I have a problem with dumb animals. Not the animals themselves you understand, but the expression. It is a general failing of humanity that when an animal or bird is easily approachable and does not flee as we appear over the horizon, we mock this creature and call it stupid or dumb. We seem unable within our hearts to form a positive slant on the creature such as it being trusting, friendly, or even endearingly naïve; which is actually surely what they actually are since they have no idea what a completely cruel and unscrupulous creature they have come up against.

Birds are considered by some to be quite the dimmest of creatures, hence the expression bird brained. It has been suggested that the ability to fly has removed the need for cleverness. In any situation that threatens the birds they will simply fly away. This particular strategy has come unravelled against the ingenuity and indifference of human beings who have devised weapons that tilt the odds heavily in the favour of themselves and with fatal consequences for the bird. This belittling of animals' intelligence is, I suspect, to allay feelings of guilt at abusing their trust and treating them so abominably. We know it's not right but somehow if something is considered dumb it is fair game, it deserves what it gets for being so stupid, it's not our fault, we are not to blame, they have brought it on themselves.

It is not just the English speaking people that have this idea that birds are less than savvy. In Spanish there is an expression *cabeza de chorlito* which literally means plover's head but translates to scatter-brained.

The name dotterel in itself seems quite quaint and innocuous, until you delve into what it actually means. It is derived from the old English word *dote*, which means simpleton or fool, indeed in Scotland the dotterel is also known as the moss fool. In Gaelic it is called *Amadan-Mòintich* ('peat-bog fool') reflecting both its perceived stupidity and its chosen environment. John Skelton (1460-1529) in his *The Book of Phillip Sparrow* (before 1508) referred to the bird thus;
  '*the Dotterell, that foolish peck*'
The scientists perpetuated this idea, nominating the bird *morinellus* meaning little fool, from the Latin *morus* meaning foolish.

These birds were regularly netted on their migration north through England. Trapping was carried out at night using a light to dazzle the birds and stones bashed together to chivvy the birds towards the waiting net. An unusual myth arose from these netting days that the birds would imitate their hunter's movements;

'Being a kind of bird as it were of an apish kind, ready to imitate what they see done, are caught according to foulers gesture: if he put forth an arme, they also stretch out a wing: sets he forward his legge, or holdeth up his head, they likewise doe theirs ; in briefe, whatever the fouler doth, the same also doth this foolish bird untill it be hidden within the net.'

(William Camden 1551 – 1623)

They were thus persecuted for sport, for the pot and for their plumage – their feathers were prized by fishermen for making trout flies – and were also sought after by egg collectors and taxidermists. Hunters would look for them at their traditional stopping-off places on the Yorkshire coast. The Dotterel Inn, where hunters would stay, still exists near Filey, while other traditional stopping places led to the naming of two Dotterel Halls in Cambridgeshire and a Dotterel Farm in North Yorkshire. It is claimed that a hunter could expect to shoot fifty pairs in a season.

There is also an old adage passed down from the shepherds referring, presumably, to the southern movements of the dotterels portending the coming of winter, much as the disappearance of the common swifts from our town fill me with a feeling that winter is not far away. However one can only assume that the birds must have been more numerous and lingered much more on their southward journey than they do now;

'When dotterel do first appear, it shows that frost is very near ;

But when the dotterel do go, then you may look for heavy snow.'

62

In Hawai'i the Pacific Golden Plover or *kōlea* has a special place in the hearts of the Hawaiians featuring heavily in local culture and customs. These birds have been making the journey between Alaska and Hawai'i for at least one hundred and twenty thousand years, according to fossil evidence, so it is clearly a survival strategy that works for them. Obviously a bird that has been around for so long, and which has caught the attention of people, is likely to be drawn into local myths and legends. This is certainly true of the *kōlea* and many of these stories still persist to this day. Some of these superstitions are positive, for example if a *kōlea* flies across your lawn you will receive a visitor, and some not so good, such as if a *kōlea* circles your house calling there will be a death in the family. That said, in Hawai'i *kōleas* are believed to be protective spirits and messengers to the high chiefs from the gods. There are traditional songs and hulas inspired by the *kōlea*. The translation of *kōlea* is 'one who takes and leaves' echoed in a Hawaiian proverb that says; '*The kōlea eats until he is fat, and then returns to the land from whence he came*' describing how they only nest in foreign lands but return to Hawai'i to fatten up. In legends, the god of healing and patron of the *kahunas*, Koleamoku, could turn himself into a *kōlea*.

The *kōlea* is cited in another story that also involves the *'Ulili* or wandering tattler. The story goes that a chief called Moloka'i kidnapped the wife of another man. He employed the services of the *kōlea* and *'Ulili* to stand guard should a rescue attempt be made. When the woman's son arrived in order to free her the birds attacked him and pulled at his hair (that'll teach him!). All very high drama for two species that are, usually, so docile.

The *'Ulili* was also considered to be a sacred messenger or scout due to its vociferous nature and being a sentinel bird that warned all others of the approach of danger. It is for that very same reason that it got its name tattler, being a tell-tale tattler.

Remaining in Hawai'i the ruddy turnstone or *'Akekeke* also enters legend as a messenger of the gods alongside the *kōlea* and *'Ulili*. It is said that Hawaiian chiefs and gods would send these intelligent and strong birds over the ocean on important assignments. Compare that to the way our ancestors thought about the dotterel and other birds. Very few, if any, stories about our birds give them praiseworthy traits.

There exists an old superstition concerning the Seven Whistlers, which were supposed to be a portent of impending doom as mentioned by William Wordsworth (1770-1850) in his poem, *Though narrow be that Old Man's cares*:

'He the seven birds hath seen, that never part,
Seen the SEVEN WHISTLERS in their nightly rounds'

The story goes that six of the Seven Whistlers travel endlessly across the night skies looking for the seventh. In days past they would often be reported passing overhead and it is widely supposed, by those of a less superstitious nature, that these whistlers were in fact Eurasian whimbrels. The legend continues that if the six should ever find the seventh whistler then the world would come to an end. So, be warned, if you should ever come across seven whimbrels anywhere, you had better get all your redshanks in a row.

However it is not just whimbrels that have had this epithet attached to them. The European golden plover is also supposed, in some parts, to carry the same burden. In his *English Folk-lore* (1878) the Rev. Thomas Firminger Thiselton-Dyer informs us that the superstition in Lancashire tells the same story as the whimbrels;

'There is a Lancashire superstition which identifies the plover with the transmuted soul of a Jew. When seven of them are seen together, they are called the 'seven whistlers,' and their sound, it is said, foretells misfortune to those who hear it. A correspondent of Notes and Queries thus alludes to this odd piece of superstition: 'One evening a few years ago, when crossing one of our Lancashire moors, in company with an intelligent old man, we were suddenly startled by the whistling over-head of a covey of plovers. My companion remarked that, when a boy, the old people considered such a circumstance a bad omen, 'as the person who heard the wandering Jews,' as he called the plovers, 'was sure to be overtaken with some ill-luck.'

The story continues that the teller of the tale, when arriving at the journey's end, missed his connection for a coach to his destination causing him to have to walk. The old man reminded him of the tale of the Seven Whistlers and added that the legend had come true.

The belief was that these birds hold the souls of those who had helped to crucify Jesus who were condemned to float in the air forever more. Hearing their call was considered to be bad luck, whereas for me I consider any day that I hear the lovely toot of a golden plover a lucky day indeed. The hearing of this plover's call was put to a more practical, if dodgy, use as a good way of getting a winter's day off work by the coal miners of Leicestershire. They believed that if the call of the golden plover was heard it was a portent of a calamity of some kind and they would steadfastly refuse to go down the pit that day. Sounds like a rather flimsy excuse for a day off to me;

'Sorry boss, can't come in today, heard a plover calling'.

'Oh! Right you are Collier, see you tomorrow - if those golden plovers in the field out the back of your house have gone by then!'

However it is not just the whimbrels and golden plovers that have been saddled with this particular burden of endless drudgery and searching. The Eurasian curlew too is suspected of being the species involving the Seven Whistlers or some ghostly huntsman attended by his hounds bringing death and ruin to those who see them and to any house over which they linger. The Scottish name for the curlew is whaup and this name has also been given to an evil spirit in Ayrshire that goes about under the eaves of houses after the fall of night, having a long beak resembling a pair of tongs for the purpose of carrying off evil doers.

In the 7th Century the grand old Welsh St Beuno was said to be sailing between Llanddwyn and Clynnog when he dropped his prayer book onto the sea. A passing curlew swooped down, scooped up the book and took it to the shore where the book was laid out to dry on some rocks. When St Beuno arrived he was so grateful he blessed the curlew and prayed for its protection.

St Beuno, however, was not the first to thus bless the curlew. Before him, in the 5th Century, St Patrick of Ireland too, legend would have it, heaped blessings on the curlew after he set sail for the Isle of Man. Having got lost in the fog it was the call of a curlew that told him in which direction to sail and that earned the bird his blessing promising that it would forever be protected and its nest hard to find.

It seems though that the passage of time is eroding the good works of these venerable gentlemen as the curlew is plummeting in numbers not only in Wales and Ireland, but across the British Isles and beyond.

Waders have also inspired the discovery of unseen, far off lands and feature in global discovery, being key players in the arrival in the 'New World' by European explorers. Legend has it that after twenty nine days sailing west across the Atlantic Ocean Christopher Columbus and the crews of his three ships were beginning to get a bit twitchy, sailing as they were into the unknown. They were desperate to find the land that they hoped would be just over the horizon, mutinous thoughts of turning back must have been on the minds of more than one of the nervous crew members.

Suddenly a great throng of birds flew into sight, masses of them, hundreds upon hundreds, thousands of birds in a flock heading in a purposeful manner and intent on some distant goal. Someone in the crew, maybe even Columbus himself, recognised these birds as being birds of the land not seabirds and therefore, they reasonably supposed, they were heading for dry land. Columbus had his helmsman swing the ship after the birds and follow in their wake. The result you could honestly say is history.

But what were these birds that they saw in such impressive numbers out over the open ocean? The description was of a vast flock of them, the like of which we imagine when talking of the Passenger Pigeon, but that species was a land lubber and they were never known to fly out over the ocean in their vast flocks. There are therefore two candidates which have migration routes that cross the Atlantic from Canada to South America at that time of year (October) that have also been reported in such enormous flights: American golden plover, which still follows the same route to this day, although in much smaller numbers, and Eskimo curlew which sadly is now almost certainly extinct. Both species would gather near the coast in north-east North America on their southward migration and then head out across the Atlantic with a view to making landfall in South America. If all went well very few of these birds would be seen along the coast but, if the weather turned, they would often be pushed back to land where massed ranks of gunners would be waiting for them and who would kill vast numbers of them in the short time that they were grounded. Eventually they would break free again and head back out to sea, bound for South America once more. It would be a cruel irony indeed if it were the Eskimo curlew which had directed the explorers to the continent, the colonisation of which, in turn, lead to their extinction.

Pacific golden plovers spend much time in flight over the sea too. Travelling as they do over the Pacific Ocean inevitably would have drawn them to the attention of seafarers.

The first of these, it has been suggested, were the ancient Polynesian people who may have been guided to the Hawaiian Islands by the Pacific golden plover as they were seen to fly north from the southern Oceanic Islands on their way back to Alaska. It could be that seeing the bird head north gave the Polynesians reason to expect land in that direction and, although modern science indicates that the birds which visit the South Pacific islands return to Alaska via Japan instead, it may have been enough to get them to set sail. Interestingly the same could be true of the first inhabitants of New Zealand as the Polynesians would have also seen many birds heading south from their islands as well.

Another seafarer, one Captain James Cook, also made the acquaintance of the Pacific golden plover. Cook sailed in search of the mythical 'Great Southern Continent' which we now know neither he, nor anyone else, was ever destined to find. During this voyage he and his crew came across a Pacific golden plover and, upon learning from the Tahitians that the bird did not nest in the region but was only a visitor, they surmised that this was possible evidence of the missing continent further to the south. On a later voyage, now seeking the north-west passage Cook found himself in the north Pacific and came across another Pacific golden plover which seemed to be migrating south, which meant that they must know exactly where the islands to the south were positioned. This prompted Cook to wonder if the birds knew more about geography and navigation than he did; which of course they did.

Returning to pagan times, once more the ubiquitous lapwing turns up in an Early Medieval alphabet called Ogham; that which is often seen inscribed upon stones from the 4th to 6th centuries. In the same way that we might say A is for Apple the users of this script, associated with Celtic traditions, would say A is for *aidhircleog*, which means lapwing, and is written as a cross. Another of the bird Oghams is the letter N for *naescu*, which is the snipe, and depicted by a vertical line with five equally spaced lines emanating from it to the right like a sparsely toothed comb.

It was not just the pagans that wove waders into their myths. The Christians have a story that when Herod's soldiers were out searching for new born babies to slay, the baby Jesus was concealed on a beach under seaweed by an oystercatcher. The bird's reward for this deed was for it to be permanently marked with the sign of the cross, which is made up of the white of its rump and tail base stretching onto the back and the white wing bars. Chronologically this doesn't make a lot of sense since the cross didn't come into Jesus' story until much later and I'm also not sure which seaweed strewn beach was the venue for this story. Another tenuous link to Jesus for the oystercatcher is that it was called, in Scotland, *Gille-Bhrighde*, or Servant of Brigid or Bride and the story goes that St Bride was the wet nurse for Jesus.

A very similar story tells of a different relationship to St Bride. It says that it was she who was running away, not from Herod's soldiers but from a band of enemies who wished to kill her. Finding herself alone and cornered on a beach she decided she was done for. She prayed to God thanking him for the life she had enjoyed and lay on the sand in anticipation of her impending death. Whereupon an oystercatcher, who just happened to be passing, realised she was in a fix and covered her with seaweed. Thus she was hidden from her pursuers and her life spared. Without further ado she blessed the oystercatcher and this is also said to be the reason an oystercatcher carries the sign of the cross in its plumage.

Do Eurasian woodcocks carry their young? Do they also give piggy back rides to goldcrests or migrate to the moon? All these ideas have carried a great deal of weight in some parts. The idea that woodcocks carry their young between their feet or perhaps between the feet and the belly is widely known and believed. There are many instances of country and shooting folk seeing this first hand and papers have been written as proof of the fact. However, there has never been any irrefutable evidence, to my knowledge, in the form of film footage or photos, only the word of unquestionably honest people. I also wonder, on the occasions when people have witnessed this event, whether the chick has inadvertently got caught up in the adult's undercarriage being transported by mistake rather than design?

The goldcrest has the colloquial name in Yorkshire of the 'woodcock's pilot'. Some have taken this to mean that when migrating across the North Sea from Europe, goldcrests, tiny and ill equipped to fly such distances alone, hitch a lift on the back of a woodcock. Whilst this is not entirely impossible it is highly unlikely but one witness account does claim seeing a short-eared owl with a goldcrest on its back coming in off the sea. The story teller caught the goldcrest but failed to shoot the owl after the smaller bird had dismounted.

It is conceivable that this is a misinterpretation of the word pilot. It clearly does not refer to an individual, in this case a goldcrest, sitting like the pilot of an aeroplane directing the woodcock's flight, since the expression predates the invention of flying machines; pilots are also individuals put aboard ships to navigate them in difficult waters.

But it may not refer to the goldcrest being aboard the bigger bird at all. It may instead take the meaning as used in a pilot vessel that guides a larger ship safely into harbour. Large falls of goldcrests on the east coast of England very often portend a similar fall of woodcocks a few days later, thus giving the impression that they have 'shown the way' to the larger birds.

With regard to migrating to the moon it was supposed that the woodcocks left us, along with other migrating birds on a journey which took them two months, to the moon. There they remained for three more months and then spent two further months returning to earth. The reason for this peculiar idea seems to be derived from a bizarre lack of recorded observations of them flying in a horizontal plane over the earth's surface.

A near relative of the Eurasian woodcock is the American woodcock, very similar in many ways with a cryptic and confusing plumage. There is an ancient lore among some indigenous American people that the Great Maker, when he or she had finished creating all the other birds, fashioned the American woodcock by using up all the pieces of other birds bird that had been left over, unused.

There is an old Chinese proverb about a fight between a snipe and a clam. It is probable that the translation should be sandpiper or oystercatcher rather than snipe since snipe do not prey on clams; nevertheless this is how it goes.

A clam was sitting out in the sun when suddenly a snipe flew down to peck at it. Abruptly the clam slammed its shell shut, gripping the snipe's beak in between. The snipe said,

'If it doesn't rain today, and it doesn't rain tomorrow, I shall see a dead clam on the beach.' The clam reposted,

'If I don't open today, and I don't open tomorrow, I shall see a dead snipe on the beach.'

While they were still grappling with each other in this stand-off, a fisherman passed by and netted them both. The moral of this tale is that if two parties are at loggerheads they can become so embroiled in their dispute that they are unaware of what is going on around them allowing some third party to come along and take advantage of the situation. The protagonists both end up losers and the third party the winner.

The interesting caveat to this tale is that there are records of waders being killed by bivalve molluscs, especially oystercatchers, when the mollusc clamps shut on the predator's bill and does not release the bird. The tide then rises and the bird drowns.

The oystercatcher's call is described in Gaelic as *bi glic, bi glic* which translated means 'be wise, be wise'. Sadly not all oystercatchers are endowed with this trait as the following folklore tale illustrates.

One day an oystercatcher was hunting limpets and found one relaxed. It thrust its beak between the shell and the rock. The limpet responded by tightening its grip on the rock trapping the bird's beak. There they remained until the tide came in and drowned the oystercatcher. The story continues that the bird called to its friends who gave it the rather unhelpful advice to hang on until the tide turned, by which time of course the bird had perished.

This must feel be a bit like being outwitted and murdered by a hamburger, however, another aside here concerns the oystercatcher and the Scottish Police College. This is based at Tulliallan Castle, in Kincardine-on-Forth, in the grounds of which there are apparently many oystercatchers. The college boasts a coat-of-arms that bears the images of two oystercatchers and the college's motto which is the Gaelic *bi glic ,bi glic.* In this case the translation is given as 'Be wise, be circumspect' a slight variation on the previous interpretation and one of which the students will be constantly reminded by their noisy oystercatcher neighbours.

Chapter Five

A miscellany of inspiration

'All over the tundra are to be found moribund patches, dead but for the plover and curlew that haunt it with their ghostly cries'

Sven Waxell (1701-1762)

The link between eggs, springtime and Easter are all pretty obvious as the three things more or less coincide in the northern hemisphere, despite Easter being a movable feast.

Northern lapwings were once tremendously common throughout the British Isles and their nests were easy to find. It became traditional to collect their eggs at Easter but inevitably, as the human population grew and the gourmands of the world discovered the delights of 'plover' eggs, the pressure on the lapwing population began to take its toll. Greater and greater demand came from the markets in London to supply this delicacy to the tables of those who could afford them. Many thousands of eggs were collected.

This was clearly not sustainable and inevitably the supply

dwindled as the lapwings started to disappear. As a result market traders looked further afield for their eggs and they started to be shipped down from the north of England, as well as the continent, to supply the rapacious demand. The problem became so acute that in the end the British Government of the day had to bring in 'Special provisions with respect to the lapwing' within the 1926 Wild Birds Protection Bill. In 1928 the Protection of Lapwing Bill made it illegal to sell lapwings or their eggs for human consumption during the breeding season. This lead to the practice dying out and lapwing numbers recovered considerably. They are now protected by The Wildlife and Countryside Act 1981.

The lapwings association with farmland and farming is further exemplified by the Farming & Wildlife Advisory Group National Silver Lapwing Award which has been awarded for over 40 years. To be the recipient of this award a farmer needs to demonstrate 'a real commitment to species and habitat conservation and be able to show how they integrate their environmental management in their overall farm business.'

Further afield, in the Province of Friesland, in the north of the Netherlands, the northern lapwing is called *ljip*. It is Friesland's regional symbol, appearing often in local culture such as in folk songs, poetry and colloquial expressions. When the collection of northern lapwing eggs had been banned across Europe, Friesland retained regulated egg collection and was the only place in Europe where they could still be collected on cultural-historical grounds. The season for collecting was set between the beginning of March until around the end of the first week in April. This collection however was not a free for all with everyone running around the countryside plundering all available lapwing nests. Each participant had to get permission from the provincial council before taking any eggs. Once the first clutch of eggs was taken the collector then had the job of protecting the second clutch, often by placing a cage over the nest to protect it from being trampled by cows or later destroyed during hay cutting. As a result few lapwings kept their first clutch but fewer were lost during the hay making process. Despite objections from bird protection groups, a total of six thousand eggs could be collected. Originally tradition had it that the first egg collected in this way would be presented to the Queen of the Netherlands. That tradition was ended in 1968, after which it was presented to the Queen's Commissioner to the region and more latterly the local mayor.

On the 7th December 2005 the Dutch Council of State ruled that the gathering of lapwing eggs in Friesland was prohibited on the grounds that it conflicted with the European directives on wild birds and the collecting ceased. There seems to have been a certain amount of toing and froing on the issue since then but from 2015 the finder of the first egg of the province and the finders of the first eggs in each of the communities are honoured by the King's Commissioner and by the mayors. The eggs cannot be taken, but must remain in their nests. When all the first eggs of the province have been reported, people are no longer allowed to enter the fields where lapwings are breeding. No-one that is except for the so-called *nazorgers*, who are a kind of caretaker for the lapwings. These people are appointed by the *Bond Friese VogelWachten* and they are allowed to enter a section of farmland that is assigned to them, with approval from the farmer. Much as in the past during the collecting days, they search for the eggs of all the meadow nesting waders such as godwits, redshanks and oystercatchers in addition to the lapwings and register them into a database. When the farmer wants to work the field, the *nazorgers* place markers to highlight the nest position so the farmer can avoid destroying the nest when mowing or carrying out other essential activities. Sometimes a cage is still placed over the nest to protect it from trampling by cows or sheep or a 'hood' may be used to protect the eggs from slurry/manure spreading operations.

There is a lot of discussion in Friesland about this thorny issue. Would the continued collection of eggs present a threat to the species? Both sides of the argument can quote studies to support their stance, but it is fair to say that the collection of the first egg is unlikely to be as pressing in terms of a threat to the species as intensive farming, the lack of hay meadows, low water levels and the increase in predator numbers.

In 2018 the first Friesian egg was found on March 16th in the southwest part of Friesland province. This first egg was followed by a second in the same nest the next day. Sadly those eggs ended up being abandoned, probably in this case due to the very cold start to spring.

Chocolate Easter eggs were first made in 1875 by the Cadbury factory, but they were not universally accepted as a traditional thing, how could they be, they were new after all? In England though the lapwings had created a 'need' among the population for eggs of some kind, special eggs, not just any old eggs, at Eastertime. This need could now only be sated by an alternative to the traditional 'plover's egg', and it needed to be a delicious alternative not just a symbolic one such as a painted hen's egg. The result was the coming together of a need for eggs and the availability of chocolate eggs which has now burgeoned into a very large business enterprise for the chocolatiers.

It is about time that these chocolatiers celebrated their debt to the lapwing by creating Easter lapwings to sell alongside their bunnies and eggs. Even I might be persuaded to fork out for one of those (especially if a proportion of the profit were to go to Wader Quest). Chocolate lapwing, anyone?

Pied avocets are undoubtedly one of the most popular and recognisable waders in the UK. They are elegant in their beauty, uncommon enough to be interesting and of course they are the great come-back story among our native birds resulting in them becoming immortalised as the RSPB symbol. This choice was inspired by the re-colonisation of England by the pied avocet and the RSPB's efforts to protect it against all comers, be they collectors or predators. The pied avocet is clearly one of the organisations biggest and highest profile success stories.

The RSPB is one of the most effective conservation organisations in the world, with a huge number of members; still rather larger than Wader Quest - but we're working on it. Recently the organisation's move away from strictly birds to a rather broader natural history mandate has been somewhat controversial. But love 'em or hate 'em their logo is unmistakeable.

Up and down the UK there are many smaller bird and ornithological groups, clubs and societies and it is interesting to note that a good number of them have selected waders as their logo.

The most common seems to be the Eurasian oystercatcher which is represented in the logos of the Isle of Mull Bird Club, the Gower Ornithological Society, the Wirral Bird Club and the Lancaster and District Birdwatching Society. The sporting folk of East Kilbride have also taken to the bird, their Rugby, Football and Cricket clubs all use the oystercatcher as their emblem.

The Northern lapwing is also very popular with the North Cotswold and Bradford Ornithological Societies, the Nuneaton and District Birdwatchers' Club and the Fylde Bird Club all selecting it. Perhaps a little more surprising, in the sense that it is less common, is the use of the little ringed plover. On the other hand if the bird is a bit special, as this bird is in many places, perhaps it is not altogether that surprising that the Wensum Valley Bird Watching Society, the Ogston Bird Club and the Swillington Ings Bird Group have all used it. In addition, the Shoreham District Ornithological Society have used this species and the common ringed plover together. The latter also appears on the logo of the South Cheshire Ornithological Society.

Locally special birds feature in the fenland Bird Clubs of Peterborough and Cambridgeshire in the form of the black-tailed godwit. Once a common species in the fens, it is now just about clinging to existence since it reappeared as a breeding bird in the 1950s. In 2017, the WWT, jointly with the RSPB, created Project Godwit to help to re-establish a viable population and it is now the subject of a headstarting programme where chicks are hatched and raised in captivity then released on fledging.

Reflecting the upland localities of the Derbyshire

Ornithological Society and the Huddersfield Bird Club, their logos feature the Eurasian curlew, a bird that is becoming more special as its numbers decline in Britain.

Wader Quest has of course adopted the whimbrel as its logo, replacing the original spoon-billed sandpiper, to better represent a wider interest in all waders, not just those that are Critically Endangered.

Closely related, and definitely the rarest representative of this group of waders on British club logos, is that of the Glamorgan Bird Club which displays the little curlew (or little whimbrel as it was once called). This is because that was the locality of the first record of the species in Britain, certainly something of which to be proud.

Another rare species, albeit one that is perhaps becoming less rare these days as it is showing signs of becoming a regular breeding bird, is the Black-winged stilt. This represents the Nottinghamshire Birdwatchers and again this was due to a British first, in this case the first breeding record that occurred in the locality in 1945.

I'm sure there are many more logos that could be dug up with diligent searching, it is not suggested that this is an exhaustive list by any means and many more may exist. These are merely a selection of the places and societies that we have come across or visited in the course of giving talks or being in the field.

Within the RSPB reserve fraternity the influence of waders goes even further than simply sharing a logo. There has been an annual competition that has been running since 2011 between

RSPB wetland reserves to see which achieves the highest tally of wader species seen. The birds have to land on managed RSPB wetlands between April and October; flyovers do not count. Clearly there are some reserves that have no chance and in truth there are really only three contenders and one of those is Minsmere the reserve created for the pied avocets; but even this is a bit of an outsider. Each year the competition, known as the 'Golden Welly', is a two horse race between neighbouring reserves across The Wash, Titchwell Marsh in north-west Norfolk and the combined Lincolnshire reserves of Frampton Marsh and Freiston Shore in Lincolnshire. The latter has won it outright three times and once shared the honours with Titchwell Marsh which held the title just once. Each year they record thirty-two to thirty-four species each. It's hard to imagine any other group of birds having the charisma to inspire inter reserve competition of this kind.

In the early 1950s, Sir Hugh Beaver and his friends were out for a day's shooting on Wexford Slobs in Ireland. During the course of the day, a Eurasian golden plover flew past at such speed that none there had time to raise their guns, much less loose off a shot at the bird. By the end of the day Sir Hugh had failed to bag a single one. This rankled him somewhat and it led to a discussion, and much conjecture, as to which of the European game birds had the swiftest flight. Surely, he suggested, it must be the golden plover?

Later that evening, and in the days that followed, scouring the literature on the subject at the time did not produce a satisfactory answer. In 1954 Sir Hugh, who was then Managing

Director of the Guinness Brewery, remembered the galling episode and was inspired to come up with the idea of creating a book that contained the superlative facts and figures of the world. It was a book he envisaged that would be placed in every pub the length and breadth of the country to settle arguments without recourse to fisticuffs. So it was that in 1955 the Guinness Book of Records, later to become Guinness World Records, was launched.

There are a number of reasons that people seem to dislike George W. Bush the ex-President of the USA, but here's one you may not have heard about before. On September the 1st 1994 on the first day of the dove hunting season in Texas, both Governor Ann W. Richards and George W. Bush, her Republican opponent, were out at the crack of dawn, to show they were the true candidates of the people by hunting (or rather shooting) doves.

This obligatory macho political rite in Texas turned into yet another huge embarrassment for Bush when he pointed a borrowed shotgun at the sky and accurately fired at the bird he had seen, felling the poor creature with just one shot, something of which he might have been proud had he not killed the wrong species of bird.

What Bush had assumed was a dove turned out to be a killdeer, which was legally protected and the killing of which is a crime under Texas state law. The maximum fine for this crime was $500 but Bush was fined just $130.

'*I've spoken to a game warden,*" he said. "*he's going to write a citation and I will pay the fine. I thought it was a dove. I made a mistake and I'm going to pay for it'*; Bush paid $130 while the killdeer paid a rather heavier price for the politician's error. Ironically Bush, who said he hunted frequently, in shooting the killdeer, broke the law just moments after a news conference in which he lambasted Richards as being soft on criminals. For her part apparently Richards fired a few shots in the air, more for show and to satisfy the gathered photographers than with any hope of felling a dove, there being no doves at which to shoot, but at least her vainglorious efforts did not result in any collateral damage to other species.

It would seem that the curlew sandpiper is not necessarily fussy when it comes to choosing a mate. A bird, which was described as a new species called 'Cox's sandpiper', was subsequently reputed to be a subspecies of pectoral sandpiper. This thinking however has now been overturned too by the use of DNA testing which shows that the bird is a hybrid between a female curlew sandpiper and a male pectoral sandpiper. In a similar fashion, there was also a species described by Baird in 1858 which was called 'Cooper's sandpiper'. This bird was collected in the USA and something very similar has also been seen in Australia, but again this has proved to be a hybrid between the good old curlew sandpiper and, in this case, a sharp-tailed sandpiper. All I can say is at least they are keeping it in the family.

One of the most distinctive features of the common sandpiper, and the one for which it is perhaps best known, is its restless habits and its teetering; the pulsating lifting and lowering of the back end of its body. An explanation for this behaviour is hard to come by but it has been suggested that it has something to do with imitating the rhythmical swash of waves on a shoreline. I am dubious about this as the habitat of this bird is not exclusively to be found along the shorelines of lakes that would have any sort of wave motion. It is just as likely to be found on streams and rivers or smaller ponds and pools which, either have a more chaotic visual movement, with random surges and splashes or, are almost completely still. But whatever the reason for this rhythmic action it has gained the bird a rather unfortunate name on the small island of Nukumanu in Papua New Guinea.

A gentleman by the name of Don W. Hadden was collecting the local names of the bird species of the North Solomon Islands while making lists of the birds for each he visited. On Nukumanu he discovered a local name for the common sandpiper which, whenever uttered, made the men folk fall about laughing and on one occasion leading them to even eject a small boy from their presence. When Hadden later showed this name to a lady she was utterly shocked and insisted he erase it forthwith but offered no explanation as to why. He later discovered that this name meant '*the bird that walks a little then copulates*' referring to the pumping motion that the bird makes. I rather suspect that the word copulate has replaced a somewhat more colourful one for describing the sex act. So what is this name? Well of course, I couldn't possibly say for fear of offending someone.

Hawaiian Airlines gave its fleet of aeroplanes names that reflect the beauty of the world around us and the skies above us.

Among those names are a number of birds known in the Hawaiian Islands and three of them are waders, all migrants, which visit the islands from the north. All the aeroplanes concerned are Boeing 767s and for those who take an interest in such things their registration numbers are recorded here so you can look out for them.

N580HA is named *Kōlea,* which, as we have seen, is the local name for Pacific golden plover. The next is N592HA, which has been given the name *Hunakai,* the Hawaiian name for the sanderling. The word actually means sea foam, as I understand it, which is an excellent and observant name for these little birds that dwell in that part of the beach where sea foam forms. The last of these aircraft is N594HA that has been named *'Ulili* after the wandering tattler.

Chapter Six

Inspirational waders

'Many species of this group are such far-ranging, graceful creatures that they seem clothed in mystery and romance. They are creatures with tremendous capacity for flight – veritable pilgrims of the air – nomads of the feathered world. Their migration is coextensive with all lands of the habitable globe, from the polar basin to the farthest extremities of the three southern continents. Their wild love songs defy description as does the perfume of the gardenia.'

Alaskan Bird Trails (1943) - Herbert Brandt: (1884 - 1955)

For some time, it had been mooted that the *baueri* race of Bar-tailed Godwit travelled from Alaska to New Zealand non-stop. This seemed unbelievable, it was such a huge distance, and yet marked birds had been seen in Alaska, then subsequently reported in New Zealand some days later, on a time scale that would surely not allow for the birds to have made a stop-over. Brief stop overs are not the norm, once a bird has halted its migration it needs time to take on more fuel and to rest. Many days, even weeks, may be involved, as rarely, if ever, do they touch and go.

It was decided to track the godwits as they travelled from Alaska to New Zealand in 2005, but these efforts failed to produce the hoped for results due to the transmitters not functioning properly. They all stopped working before any of the birds had even departed from Alaska. Some of these birds however were later seen alive and well in New Zealand and Australia proving that the birds had not been adversely affected by the transmitters as some had feared, the fault lay with the transmitters themselves. But the conundrum of how they got to their destinations was unresolved and the conjecture continued.

In 2006 a rather more successful attempt was made and one bird was tracked to within 100 km of New Zealand when disappointingly its transmitter stopped. This means it *probably* flew non stop from Alaska to New Zealand but, scientifically speaking, *probably* is not good enough.

A further satellite tagging scheme to track the birds' return route north via the Yellow Sea was hatched in 2007. This time the plan was to confirm where and how the bar-tailed godwits of New Zealand stopped-over on their journey back to Alaska.

Of several godwits fitted with transmitters, one was a female known affectionately as E7, due to the leg flag with which she had been adorned by researchers. Unbeknown to all concerned, this elegant bird was soon to be catapulted to fame.

E7 flew non-stop for nearly seven and a half days, to reach the Yellow Sea at an average speed of approximately 56 km per hour. E7's flight ended at Yalu Jiang Nature Reserve and became the longest ever recorded for a migratng land bird, 10,219 km. She remained there for six weeks, while she refuelled and rested, ready for the next part of her journey back to Alaska. After her rest and recuperation stop she returned to Alaska, a further 6,459 km to the north-east, again in a non-stop, six day, epic flight.

This though is when things started to drift into the realms of fantasy for the scientists. The batteries in the transmitters that had been fitted to E7, and the others, had a supposed life sufficient to get them to the Yellow Sea and then, possibly, on to the Alaskan breeding grounds. Some of the batteries faded and died as expected but surprisingly E7's transmitter, along with a few others kept working. (They must have been those special batteries that are shoved up the backsides of tambourine playing, pink bunnies of the adverts on television - other batteries are available.)

Eventually, when the breeding season finished in late July E7 left her nesting area with her transmitter still sending signals. The scientists watched as E7 flew to the coast where the bar-tailed godwits gather to build up strength and supplies for their southward migration.

One day, towards the end of August, she left. The scientists, and a growing number of fans on the internet, watched with their hearts in their mouths. What would happen? Would the battery keep going and finally reveal the secrets of this bird's migration? It did, and while some were utterly amazed, others were less so, having suspected as much already. As they watched, the bird flew a staggering 11,680 km, in one continuous flight of over eight days duration, non-stop back to New Zealand.

This placed E7 into the record books once more as the longest distance recorded in a single flight by a land bird. The incredible thing was that the proof was gathered more or less by chance due to a battery outlasting its normal lifespan. (See map p103.)

The last we heard E7 was still alive, albeit now with only one leg and a crooked neck, though she was no longer travelling back and forth between Alaska and New Zealand. She had retired to the Maketu Estuary and was often seen on the Pukehina Spit. The last sighting that we know of was on the 14th of September 2014 seven years after her banding date.

The disturbing caveat to this tale is that this research has revealed that most, if not all, of the *baueri* godwits that breed in Alaska migrate north via the Yellow Sea. If this is indeed true, and if the destruction of intertidal habitat in that region were to continue at the pace at which it has been, it is very possible that the entire Alaskan godwit population could be wiped out. They would not have the important staging areas that are so necessary for them to complete a successful migration. If a species cannot return to its breeding grounds and reproduce itself, it is doomed to extinction. A sobering thought.

Orange/Green Yellow/Red (OG-YR) is a plover apart. This individual is a member of the species known as shore plover that lives in New Zealand. Formerly this bird was quite widespread mainly around the coast of South Island. However, the introduction of mammalian predators, coupled with habitat destruction and disturbance, soon saw the species pushed off the main islands, leaving a small population remaining on Rangatira, an island in the Chatham group.

In an attempt to prevent the species becoming extinct, a captive breeding programme was established in the 1990s at the

National Wildlife Centre at Pukaha Mount Bruce and at the Isaac Conservation and Wildlife Trust in Peacock Springs, Christchurch. From these centres captive bred individuals are taken and released onto predator free islands on which, hopefully, they will establish new colonies.

OG-YR was one such bird. Once he had fledged at Peacock Springs he was translocated and released on Mana Island, near Wellington, on North Island. It seems though that OG-YR was unimpressed by his new home and soon left, flying back to the mainland and, after a couple of brief stops, incredibly, he was found running up and down the concrete strip alongside the aviary in which he was born, trying to get back in! The Peacock Springs staff duly obliged him and now OG-YR, the original homing plover, is once again part of the captive breeding population.

Interestingly some wild shore plovers exhibited the same homing instinct when some adult birds were translocated from Rangatira to a new island in order to establish a new colony. The birds had other ideas and returned to Rangatira even before the scientists' boat did!

Very few individual birds have a book written about them. Moonbird however, was destined for fame the moment he was caught in Rio Grande, Tierra del Fuego as an adult in 2001 by Patricia M. González and had the identification flag B95 attached to his left tibia. He was part of a study of the *rufa* subspecies of red knot that migrates from the Arctic to pass the northern winter in southern Argentina.

Moonbird was either seen, or captured, on his regular stop

over points, in places such as San Antonio Bay in Argentina and Delaware Bay in the USA, whilst travelling between his breeding grounds on an island in the north of Hudson Bay and his southerly wintering grounds. Red knots live for an average of around four or five years but Moonbird passed the average age and kept appearing year after year until he reached the ripe old age of twenty two, when he was last seen. This made him the longest living red knot on record at that time.

But why was he called Moonbird? Was it to do with migrating at night perhaps? Or was it that he always set off at full moon? Well no, it was all about maths and distances travelled. From the Arctic to Patagonia and back is around 20,000 miles or 32,000 km. Given his age and the number of journeys he has made it was calculated that he had flown the equivalent of a trip to the moon and half way back again; no mean feat for a bird that weighs just a few grams and is about the size of a thrush. Moonbird became a true star of the avian world, even to the extent that the city of Rio Grande, in Argentina, named him as a 'Natural Ambassador' for the city 'to symbolise the care and respect by its citizens for their environment.' (Map p104)

A male Red-necked phalarope that bred in Shetland, UK, also wrote itself into the history books due to its migration. It was never given a name or anything so anthropomorphic, but it did astonish the researchers that placed a geolocator on its leg. It was adorned with this leg furniture during the breeding season in 2012.

Outside the breeding season, apart from brief appearances on migration, red-necked phalaropes are largely seafarers spending their time feeding on plankton on the sea's surface. Exactly where the birds that breed in the UK do that was uncertain. The closest known winter population of red-necked phalaropes to the UK occurs in the Arabian Sea, where birds from Scandinavia are known to overwinter. It was largely assumed therefore that the British birds also might take their break from the cold in the same region. To find out if this was the case, geolocators were placed on ten birds on Fetlar in Shetland. The following year, three of the tagged birds returned. One of the drawbacks of geolocators is that in order to retrieve the data the bird has to be recaptured, the tag removed and the data analysed. In this case, of the three returning birds first spotted, just one, a female, still had its geolocator and the researchers could not catch it. After a while however, a different male bird, which also had a geolocator, was found sitting on eggs. He was recaptured and the tag removed. The expectation was that the analysis would prove what had been suspected, that the bird wintered in the Arabian Sea, but the results were much more startling.

The data on the tag showed that on leaving Shetland on the 1st of August, instead of heading south-east, the bird headed west, crossing the Atlantic in six days. Unlike many other migratory birds of course phalaropes can always stop for a rest on the sea. The bird then slowly headed south along the Atlantic coast of North America and into the Caribbean. By this time it was early September.

A little over a month later he was in the Pacific Ocean somewhere between the Galapagos Islands and Ecuador. There he spent the following five months feeding on plankton brought to the surface by the upwelling of the Humboldt Current, in a place where it has already been established that many of North America's phalaropes spend their non-breeding months. The return journey took a similar route but was accomplished in a much shorter time (although the battery ran out before it arrived) demonstrating how much more urgent the migration north is due to the imperative to breed, when compared to the more languid southerly post breeding flights. The total journey was around 22,000 km which is considerably longer than the supposed route to the Arabian Sea and it might go some way to explaining where the large numbers of red-necked phalaropes that migrate south along the east coast of North America end up.

Further research will be interesting, to see if this was a one off or the norm for the Shetland breeders which would make them part of the North American population rather then the Scandinavian population as previously assumed. Either way, this bird's journey has certainly inspired some head scratching among ornithologists.

Rocky was no ordinary piping plover, he was different. Rocky is a rather peculiar name for a plover as it conjures up tough, pugilistic pictures in the mind while piping plovers are soft, gentle, round, cuddly creatures. But it was not because of an ebullient nature that this bird had earned its name.

Rocky hatched out of his egg in 2004 much as any other piping plover before him or indeed since. He looked the same, fed the same, migrated the same in fact behaved the same in every way as all other piping plovers except when it came to breeding time on Sleeping Bear Dunes National Lakeshore, Michigan, USA, when his uniqueness manifested itself.

In his first breeding year Rocky paired up with a female. He made a little scrape which his chosen mate inspected and found to her liking and in it she placed, after the usual biological shenanigans, four precious piping plover eggs. All was going according to plan thus far. However, Rocky took one look at the wonderful egg-filled nest and decided that it was so good he just had to have one of his own. He went through the business of making a second scrape, alongside the first. Without the aforementioned biological shenanigans though, try as he might, no eggs were forthcoming. What was he to do? He cast about him and spied, lying among the pebbles, four egg-shaped rocks and these, by shuffling them along between his legs with his bill, he contrived to place in his scrape.

When it came to the parental change-over for incubation duties a problem became apparent. Rocky incubated his four rocks when it was his turn and only when it was the turn of the female did the authentic eggs get incubated. In many species it is necessary for both parents to brood their eggs if they are to have a chance of hatching, and piping plovers are among those species. As a result the researchers stepped in and removed the eggs. Of those eggs only one survived due to the lack of attention that Rocky had paid his potential offspring.

The researchers, now mindful of Rocky's shortcomings, decided that if he pulled the same trick the following season they would rear the eggs in captivity. Piping plovers are a rare breed and any unnecessary loss of progeny was to be avoided.

When springtime came in Michigan the following year, so did the piping plovers and among them was Rocky. The researchers kept a close eye on him and watched as he produced a scrape in which his mate placed another four precious piping plover eggs. Rocky was again impressed, but this time instead of creating his own version, he decided that the nest was just missing a certain something. He cast about him once again and found a single egg-shaped rock which he then manoeuvred into the nest to join the four eggs. Now, when the female sat she brooded four eggs... and a rock, and when Rocky brooded his rock he also brooded the four eggs.

The good news is all four eggs hatched; the rock however did not.

After those first two years Rocky forgot about the rocks and became an exemplary father. He returned to breed for nine years but has not been seen since and is presumably no longer with us. Piping plovers live to a maximum of around seventeen years, so Rocky could potentially have carried on producing young for a few more years. Life in the wild though, especially for small birds such as Rocky, is hazardous and living to a ripe old age is unusual.

The following account is an example of the ability of birds which are facing adversity at every turn to surprise us by overcoming somewhat staggering odds. It comes from New Zealand and concerns the black stilt which is widely known by its Māori name of *kakī*.

This bird was very close to extinction due to habitat loss and the introduction of exotic mammalian predators to New Zealand from which it had no defence. The result has been a catastrophic failure to reproduce successfully. A programme of captive breeding was instigated, and has been running for many years. As a result the wild population is gradually growing. For those in the wild reproduction is very tough, it is nothing short of a miracle for a pair to raise even one of their chicks to fledging age, so the population is being maintained by the captive breeding scheme.

In January 2017, Jemma Welch, who monitors the breeding success of birds nesting on the Tasman River, came across some recently fledged stilts and was surprised to see four together. Seeing an adult black stilt with the chicks she assumed that the other half of the pair would be a white-headed stilt or perhaps a hybrid cross between the two species. Hybridisation is not uncommon between white-headed and black stilts due to the latter being so few and far between that they are often unable to find one of their own kind with which to breed. Jemma was greatly surprised then, and wholly delighted, to see that the second bird in the pairing was also a black stilt, and better still, both sported the colour leg bands that confirmed they were both pure bred black stilts. The male bore the combination black,yellow,yellow/red,black and was nearly four years old having been released as a sub adult while the female bore the combination black,white,black/yellow,red and was a little over three years old having been released as a juvenile. Neither bird had been seen since the previous July so they had clearly been very busy in some descrete location in the meantime.

If the chances of raising just one of your clutch of four eggs to fledging age in the wild is nothing short of a miracle, then think what odds these two had overcome to raise all four through the most vulnerable period in a young stilt's life. This success story is unprecedented. However with the predator control that is being carried out in the region and the difficulty in finding every wild nest, clearly demonstrated here, there is a chance that these inspiring birds will not be a one off, but will be pioneers, the beginnings of a wild breeding recovery. Either way this is a pair of super parents.

At the time of writing, among waders, the species that holds the longevity record, according to the BTO list, is the Eurasian oystercatcher. One British bird is known to have lived for forty-one years, one month and five days. Sadly it was found 'hunted' in France in September 2017 ('freshly dead within a week'). It had originally been ringed by the Wash Wader Ringing Group in Friskney, Lincolnshire on July 30th 1976. However this records is topped by an oystercatcher in Europe that was killed by a raptor at the age of forty-three years, four months.

Where records stand, there are other waders that live for over thirty years but no other species reaches forty. The long-lived also rans include the Eurasian curlew, which has been recorded at thirty-two years and seven months exactly, and a bar-tailed godwit that reached thirty-three years, eleven months and thirteen days.

A few species reach their twenties, mainly the larger, more robust species such as pied avocet, grey plover, Eurasian whimbrel and black-tailed godwit. But some smaller ones have lived surprisingly long lives. A red knot has been recorded at twenty-seven years, three months and twenty-nine days thus toppling Moonbird from the top spot by a few years (albeit a different subspecies). A dunlin reached an amazing twenty-eight years, ten months, a very long span for such a small migrant bird living in such hazardous circumstances.

The longevity record for Eurasian woodcock is, by

contrast, just fifteen years and six months. It is a chunky, hardy bird and I wonder if they would be recorded living much longer if they were one day to find themselves not on the shooters' quarry list?

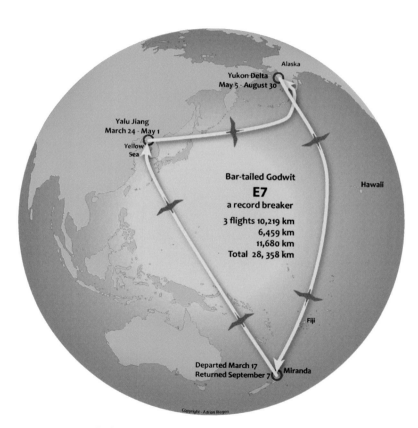

E7's migration route; see pages 91-94.

Red knot, B95 Moonbird's migration route; see pages 95-96.

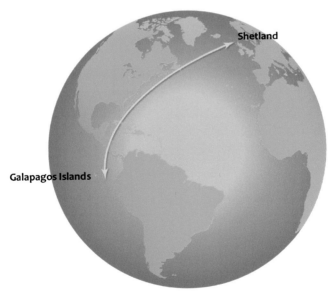

Red-necked phalarope's migration route; see pages 96-98.

Chapter Seven

An inspiration of waders

'*A cloud of birds bursts from a seemingly deserted mudflat. With uncanny synchrony, several thousand shorebirds swirl about, twisting and turning as one entity – truly one of nature's awe-inspiring spectacles*'.

The Shorebird Guide (2006) - Michael O'Brien, Richard Crossley and Kevin Karlson

What would you call a mixed or unidentified aggregation of wader species swirling in flight over your favourite estuary? What collective noun could do justice to these spectacular formations of birds tied together by invisible threads wheeling, swishing and pirouetting over an estuary when they rise up with a thunderclap of simultaneous wing beats like dry leaves lifted from a woodland floor by a sudden rush of wind.

Once up they get into formation immediately and dash headlong, low over the water, as one. As you watch a wave action may then begin like a ribbon fluttering in the wind and myriad white dots merge into one living being, thousands upon thousands of birds and twice as many beating wings. Suddenly the squadron leader banks and a millisecond later the next follows suit, and the next, then the next as a ripple rolls down the hoard. The hitherto white birds, now dull, grey-brown, all but disappear against the low cloud on the horizon then, as if by magic, they just as suddenly reappear. They spiral upwards like laughter in an empty room in one homogeneous block. As they shoot skywards they form a towering biomass of life which suddenly collapses like a burst balloon full of water and they flow out across the surface of the sea forming a living stream. Next they turn through one hundred and eighty degrees and speed back towards the beach having taken on a tubular form; they perform a victory barrel roll like half of the double helix in the DNA belonging to some unimaginably immense being. They circle once, then again, gaining height in a blizzard of thrashing wings, flickering from dark to light like a fancy illuminated bill board in Times Square. The form morphs from globular mass to undulating string recalling a massive caterpillar traversing the estuary. They then ride up to form a dancing cobra whose head breathtakingly disappears down its own throat to form a darting arrow as though they have been shot from Cupid's bow towards the very heart of the estuary. At last the frantic thrashings segue seamlessly into a more tempered urgency. Quelling their fervour, like a cat that has lost interest in a new toy, the birds become more relaxed and form a gliding cloud over their chosen roost spot. Then, as with an unexpected April shower, it starts to rain waders as they tumble and whiffle out of the sky. Plunging vertically downward they pull up at the last moment to cruise in level flight over the heads of their fellow acrobats that had alighted moments before them. Finding a space they swell the front of the congregation as they land and settle slowly into a sizzling pancake of excited birds like the head of a living, breathing lava flow. Slowly they cool and became still and quiet once more, as though this miracle of natural finesse has never happened at all.

The tide now drops and the birds begin to leave and spread across the expanding mud as the sea inhales, sucking its lapping edge back towards its inner core. Suddenly, with the roar like a jet engine not ten feet above your head another phalanx of waders flies from their roost site to join the joyous celebration of life, to be lived for another day, out over the estuary.

Even if you have experienced this many times before, each time it is different; an infinite number of shapes and forms painted like a living fresco in the vaulted ceiling of the cathedral skies above you. Just sitting there, in awe of this exuberant demonstration of the power and beauty bestowed upon the natural realm around us, it becomes clear that a world that did not contain such events would be an impoverished one indeed. Each of those birds will soon be risking everything to return to their breeding grounds to try, against the odds, to replace themselves before they die, simply to maintain their species.

So I ask again, what do you call this inspiring phenomenon? The most likely answer I would expect to hear would be a flock of waders since there is, as yet, no specific collective noun for these mixed or unidentified massed ranks of waders. Given all that has been written in the foregoing chapters of this book I put it to you that when you come across a multitude of them dashing as one, living being over the estuary, describing impossible turns and manoeuvres, flashing from dark to light as they go, that, referring to them as a flock is inadequate. That collective noun may be suitable for a bunch of random sheep on a hillside or an unruly gang of pigeons in a town square, but surely not noble or expressive enough for our majestic waders.

What about calling it a murmuration, usurping the collective noun for European starlings? That is overtly wrong. It would be no less wrong to usurp a noun that is used for other wader species, one that the individual species has inspired us to select, invent or adopt (see Appendix I). Some of which are blindingly obvious, such as a pack of knots, some are rather insulting like a deceit of lapwings, and others are entirely mystifying: witness an omniscience of godwits. We have collective nouns for many things, but somehow, one of the most striking and spectacular of life's experiences with waders has hitherto gone unrecognised in this way.

Is this because we cannot be sure exactly what we are watching? What species make up these swirling gyrations? Often they may be just one species, maybe they are all knots, in which case we could call it a pack, but can we be sure when watching so many birds at once that they are all the same? It might be that those knots are actually dunlins, or knots and dunlins, in the thousands of beating wings some may actually be attached to godwits and plovers, be they common ringed or grey. Perhaps, unnoticed a few sanderling and ruddy turnstones are scooped up in the throng around the periphery or lost in the middle of the heaving mass of birds; now they defy our attempts to give them a name, and so it seems we have never tried; except, we understand, someone once referred to them as a wedge of waders, which is hardly descriptive of the flowing beauty of these gatherings.

Surely this is a phenomenon that deserves better? It is one of nature's most engaging and breath-taking experiences to sit beside an estuary and witness this tableau in motion.

This book is an entreaty to the world at large to give this amazing spectacle a name. What you have read within its pages is not designed nor intended to be a full coverage of how waders have inspired us over the years, they are just examples to emphasise the point. Together these snippets have, I hope, encouraged you to give greater recognition to this most wonderful group of eclectic birds and their flights of fantasy, one of the natural world's greatest phenomena.

So what are we to call this mixed or unidentified group of waders speeding above the ebbing and flowing estuary waters? May I humbly submit that such magical gatherings of the birds that have been inspiring us since we came down from the trees, should be respectfully and reverently referred to as... *an inspiration of waders*'. I rest my case.

Appendix I

Collective nouns

BS

Collective nouns are a peculiarity of the English Language; other languages don't appear to indulge in them with the same enthusiasm that we seem to in the UK. In the bird world there are some crackers; a charm of goldfinches, a murder of crows and one of my favourites an exaltation of larks spring to mind. A number of waders have also attracted the attention of those that like to apply these constructed appellations.

I have already covered the collective noun, a deceit of Lapwings, in chapter four *Inspiring Myths and Legends* because there are many myths and legends surrounding this bird and how this terrible idea that they are deceitful may have arisen.

There are a number of collective nouns for other members of the plover family too, birds which are every bit as, if not more, deceitful than lapwings. Some of these nouns are a little strange and others seem very reasonable. One in the latter category to my mind is a band of plovers. This is partly because it sounds like a band of brothers which has a strong feeling of solidarity about it. These plucky little birds do give the impression of comradeship when the stand together facing the wind, and the world, in a defiant way.

On the other hand, they may be deep in thought (if plovers are capable of such things) which would give credence to ponderence [sic] and concentration as alternatives. Semipalmated plover is called *batuira-do-bando* due to being encountered mainly in small groups (*bando* translates more or less to gang, in a non-organised crime sort of way). It may also be an oblique reference to the fact that they have a distinctive band across their chests in many cases. Another is a wing of plovers and certainly in flight these birds can put on an impressive display twisting and turning with the best of them. Other plover nouns of which I have heard tell are; a brace, a flight, a leash, a stand and a trip, the last of which is most widely used for Eurasian dotterels. One that is intriguing is an invisibleness of plovers. It is true that common ringed plovers, when they stand still on a pebbled beach, can be very hard to see until they move and the mountain plover has the nick-name of 'prairie ghost' as it has the uncanny ability to disappear before your very eyes, even on open ground. The collective noun for killdeer is a season due, possibly, to deer having a season in which they can be killed?

There are a couple more plover nouns that I have come across that are clearly very apt, but, I suspect, they are from the pen of a wag rather than having any deep cultural connection. These are a range of mountain plovers and a flurry of snowy plovers; the latter is widely used among those who work to protect the species.

A slightly puzzling collective noun is that for godwits, which is an omniscience. I cannot imagine a situation where someone would cast their eyes over a throng of godwits and think, 'that lot know everything there is to know about everything'. So where does this come from? Perhaps it has something to do with the family name having the word God in it, along with the word wit, maybe referring to the wit of God, who is, by all accounts, omniscient? Since the Anglo- Saxon verb for 'to know' is *witten* there may be something in this idea. Having said all that, the name godwit is mooted to have had nothing to do with religion, or cleverness with words. It may be due to them being good to eat; *god* = good and *wit* derives from the old English word *with*, *wight* or *witha* meaning an animal of some kind. In the past, reference was often made to the delicious taste and texture of black-tailed godwit meat and this species was hunted in large numbers in England, and elsewhere no doubt, for the table. Some were even caught alive and fed until plump for special occasions. The alternative collective nouns for these birds are equally unfathomable and also have a link to religion; a prayer and a pantheon.

Eurasian curlews are known to roost together at night arriving at dusk and leaving at dawn which would certainly indicate an origin for their collective noun – a curfew of curlews; one can almost imagine them flying in as though keen to meet a curfew imposed upon them by Mother Nature. However it may also refer to the bird's propensity for calling at night, although logically that would be defying any supposed curfew placed upon them. However, the cynical among us have suggested that someone somewhere has merely looked through a lexicon of some sort and found the similarity of the two words irresistible. Another collective noun for curlew is a head. Now this surely has something to do with curly locks as another, presumably related, name is a salon. Herd and skein are also to be found and rather speak for themselves, and lastly game which must be of hunting origin.

Avocets have been saddled with colony as their collective noun. Whilst this is very apt as they do prefer the protection of this nesting system it is rather unimaginative. However, they also are known as an orchestra which is strange as they are not, at least in my view, particularly known for their musical attributes.

I have yet to get to the bottom of a parcel of oystercatchers. I looked high and low and spent many a sleepless night searching for a lateral thread that may join the two, but to no avail, except that many seafood dishes are wrapped in parcels. I suspect though it merely refers to the meaning of parcel being a group, gang or collection of something. A stew suggests that oystercatchers may be good to eat although in his book *British Birds in their Haunts* the Reverend Johns wrote; '*I was once induced... to have one served up for dinner... But I did not repeat the experiment preferring fish pure and simple to fish served up through the medium of a fowl.*' On the other hand Charles Dixon claimed; '*Its flesh, as I can testify, is not at all unpalatable, especially to a hungry sportsman amidst the wilds of the Outer Hebrides*'. A Rockefeller of oystercatchers is undoubtedly connected with food, but not in the sense of the oystercatcher being consumed but rather usurping the name of an oyster dish known as oyster Rockefeller, which comprises oysters spread with a mixture of spinach, butter, seasonings, and bread crumbs, the whole lot then being baked together on one half of the shell. No oystercatchers were harmed in the production of this dish.

Sandpipers, in particular the dunlin, have been given a fling. At first it is not obvious why this should be but watch a small group of dunlins on the shoreline, during the short dashing flights (flight is also given as a collective noun for this species) that they undertake to evade a marauding dog or passing peregrine. At these moments they certainly do fling themselves from side to side especially when trying to decide where to alight with a degree of safety. Alongside these dunlins you may come across a small collection of sanderlings. These have been nominated as a grain of sanderlings, which is cute if nothing else so therefore rather befitting of this eminently admirable little bird. Other sandpiper collective nouns include a bind and a cluster as they stick together I assume, and also, incomprehensively, a contradiction and a time-step. In the UK, small sandpipers are often referred to as stints and a spell of stints is rather amusing. In the USA, the stints' counterparts are known as peeps, and they too have their own collective noun, an enigma; western and semipalmated spring to mind, or Baird's and white-rumped perhaps, since they are difficult to separate? Another is a litter and my favourite is a diary of peeps a reference surely to Samuel Pepys diaries of 1660 - 1669.

A well-known collective noun for one of our most familiar sandpipers, a pack of knots, is widely used. These birds are often seen roosting, outside the breeding season, in large, densely formed flocks which are tightly packed together. However, imaginative minds have come up with a tangle of knots, although the flocks do not look particularly disorganised and, even when taking off in panic, I have never seen them get entangled as each occupies its own space in a perfect display of structured disorder or perhaps unstructured order?

Other Scolopacids with their own collective nouns are the quaint, whisper of tattler's and for surfbirds the rather more exciting connection to crashing waves and suntanned bodies with, a board and a *kahuna*, the latter being a surfing term for a very large wave.

A number of ruffs together is known as a hill, but it really refers to the lekking ground of the birds where the males fight ferociously for the attentions of the females in the breeding season rather than to the birds themselves. The alternative is a reference to an item of clothing and their flamboyant adornments, a collar of ruffs.

Phalaropes have collected a number of collective nouns such as a swirl, a twirl, a whirl and a whirligig all of which refer to their famous habit of picking rapidly at the surface of the water as they spin. Although this spinning is much talked about and often referred to it is actually not all that common. Phalaropes are much more likely to be seen swimming along picking at the surface of the water dipping their head from side to side, which has perhaps earned them the dopping of phalaropes collective noun, coming from dipping, describing their head movements. This action has also resulted in the Icelandic colloquial name of 'writing birds'. Whether this is because the action reminds the Icelanders of hand writing action I can't say. It doesn't have the fluidity of handwriting, but in Icelandic, with all the alphabetical characters they utilise, perhaps it is a rather more staccato action than say, in English where just cross the odd t and dot the odd i. However to my mind the random jabbing at the surface is much more reminiscent of someone poking at a typewriter or, for those more up to date, a keyboard, with one finger, much as I do. A further collective noun for phalaropes is a cell, and perhaps that may derive from the fact that flocks of these birds can be encountered, often miles out to sea, where they gather to feed, frequently in huge numbers, on plankton brought to the surface by upwelling from the depths caused by a convergence of currents.

The common snipe is notable in that it has a different collective noun for when they are on the ground – a walk, when they are in the air – a wisp and even when they have been slaughtered – a couple. As I understand it this latter is peculiar as, if you have shot more than two snipe, the noun remains the same, a couple, but the number is referred to in denominations of a couple, so, four birds would be two couple of snipe and five would be two and a half couple: the equivalent of this in other game birds is a brace. But, as would be expected of a bird so much in the line of fire it also has a number of alternatives to those three; a leash (in common with plovers) a whisper, a winnowing (referring to its display) and a volley the latter of which must also be connected to the shooting of these lovely little birds.

Whilst we are on the subject of snipe, as a slight diversion from the collective noun theme, they have been responsible for inspiring a couple of new words in the English vocabulary. '*Unfurl yourselves under my banner, noble savages, illustrious guttersnipes*', wrote Mark Twain sometime around 1869. Twain was among the first writers to use guttersnipe for a youngster of lowly status. Others in the late 19th century adopted the expression giving it the more literal use for common snipes which was probably first used from around 1875, the link being that snipe feed in the gutters and troughs to be found in wetlands. Another word has been introduced into the English language due to the snipe's reputation for being difficult to shoot. In the 19th Century British soldiers in India referred to someone as a sniper if they were handy with a gun and being a marksman who was thought skilful enough to shoot a snipe, a notoriously difficult quarry! Today the word is still used to refer to a sharp shooter although it is unlikely that a snipe would be the object of a sniper's attentions today referring more narrowly to a marksman who picks off human targets from a hidden position.

Returning to the collective noun theme, another bird that does not escape the attentions of the shooting fraternity, is the Eurasian woodcock. One such noun is a roding of woodcock. This refers to the display which is usually done singly or in pairs so is not really a collective noun, more a description of behaviour; having said that how often do you see more than two or three together anyway, as they are hardly a typical flock species. However, the following have also been mooted as collective nouns for woodcock; a cord, a covert, a covey, a fall, a flight, a plump (presumably as they are good eating when fat) and a rush. This last may be referring to the speed with which they vacate an area when disturbed by jinking rapidly between the trees.

To finish this section I offer you perhaps my favourite collective noun, which is one that is surely tongue in cheek, if not a little crude, and that is an incontinence of yellowlegs.

Appendix II

Spoony ditty

He is a spoon-billed sandpiper, he has a funny beak.
He's delicate and tiny, and relatively weak.
He lives in Arctic Russia, and winters up the creek.
It is the spoon-billed sandpiper, which we are off to seek.

Vladmir the spoonie, has a lot that's full of strife,
Every day a challenge, just fighting for his life.
His only son was butchered, by a hunter with a knife
And last year down in Myanmar, they barbequed his wife!

The detectives went to Myanmar, to gather up the facts.
They worked their little socks off, pushing to the max.
They spoke to all the chiefs there, and entered into pacts,
Turned hunters into fishermen, so spoonies could relax.

The gang went up to Russia, for spoonies they did look.
They looked and looked, then looked some more, and even
sleep forsook.
They searched in all the crevices, each cranny and each nook.
Finally they found a nest, and all four eggs they took!

Chorus
Spoonie, spoonie, what you gonna do?
Now that down in Asia there is no room for you?
Spoonie, spoonie, what you gonna do?
I hear that down in Myanmar they still make spoonie stew!

The chicks were hatched in Russia, then to England they did fly.
Not that they used their own wings, but that is by-the-by,
In comfort, peace and sanctuary, that money couldn't buy,
These chicks grew into juveniles so dapper and so spry.

So safe and warm and free from harm, the spoonies lived a
dream,
But in four walls they languished, with the captive breeding
team.
A flock was made and added to, success, so it would seem,
The captive breeding programme, was at full head of steam.

Meanwhile back in Russia, they were still denuding nests.
Hatching eggs and rearing young, free from harm or pests.
The little birds were all kept warm, with little woolly vests,
With vet on hand in case of ill, but they passed all the tests.

Then came the time to free them, to the wild they were re-
turned,
The project was a huge success, with many lessons learned.
The spoonies flew off southward, and although they were con-
cerned,
The gang could now put up their feet, a cup of tea well earned.

Chorus

Now Vladimir goes flying, with new mates on the block
It's still a challenge getting there, but he still loves Bangkok
On his way to Myanmar, where he's in for a shock
No more spoonies in the pot, just smelly fish and stock!

The moral of this ditty, says WWT,
Is if you care enough it seems, what you wish can be.
Though spoonie isn't safe yet, with help it will be free
And then my great grand-children, can see one just like me.

Chorus variation
Spoonie, spoonie, what you gonna do?
Now Asia is much safer, a place where you can rest.
Spoonie, spoonie, what you gonna do?
We hope you have a peaceful time, with love from Wader
Quest.

©Rick Simpson October 2012

Appendix III

About Wader Quest

Waders are facing some acute problems with populations of many species in steep decline across the world. Many of these species depend upon wetlands, an environment which is undergoing serious depletion the world over.

One of the wetland environments most at risk at the moment are mudflats and estuaries, the intertidal zone, which is looked upon as wastelands just waiting to be turned into something more useful like an industrial estate or an aquaculture farm.

It is often erroneously thought that birds that depend on such resources for feeding and resting, especially long distance migrants, will simply go elsewhere if they find their usual stop-over points gone, but they can't and they don't. Long distance migration is a finely tuned event that has, over the millennia, been honed so that a given individual of a species can set off at optimal weight and muscle to fat ratio, with reduced internal organs, and arrive exactly where it needs to be. They don't choose their destinations from a brochure; they are hard wired to arrive there automatically. When they arrive at that destination they need to feed and rest immediately to recover and then feed up for the next stage of the journey. If they arrive and find there is nothing to eat and nowhere to rest they do not have a reserve tank from which they can draw unused pools of energy to look elsewhere; if they can't rest and feed they die, it is as simple as that. In any case, the next suitable bit of habitat will already be holding its carrying capacity so there will be no room for more birds to thrive and survive.

But waders are not just facing problems on the mudflats. Drainage of wetlands and marshes, damming and diversion of rivers, creation of ports, marinas and airports, changes in farming practices and annual rhythms, increased use of pesticides and fertilizers, over-harvesting of shellfish and other benthic creatures, hunting - both recreational and subsistence, afforestation of savannahs, increased livestock grazing and recreational activities on beaches and coastal resorts are all having a terrible effect on the populations of many species of wader, in as many habitats as they inhabit. On top of this there is also the uncertainty of what climate change will bring to all environments across the surface of the planet.

These declines are not being caused by a rash of large, major impact, environmental disasters although some can be laid at that particular door. Most are being driven by small, apparently insignificant losses, which occur over a wide area often without attracting attention. Take the northern lapwing for example. In the last thirty years eighty per cent of the British contingent has disappeared. The Irish population of the Eurasian curlew has declined by ninety-seven per cent. This is a piecemeal loss of favourable habitat here and there having a devastating effect on the population. Just because an environmental disaster doesn't all happen at the same time, in the same place, doesn't mean it is any less of a disaster.

Wader Quest started out as a single issue fundraising effort, to raise money for the WWT spoon-billed sandpiper captive breeding programme at Slimbridge as described in Chapter one.

As we travelled our eyes were opened to so many other problems beyond that of the spoon-billed sandpiper; a marina proposal in a secluded shallow cove, forests being planted in savannahs, local developers chewing up coastal habitat at tourist destinations, beaches festooned with vehicles, disturbance caused by recreational activities such as kite surfing, dog walking, horse riding, picnicking, barbeques and much more, everywhere we went. Many localised tragedies are squeezing out the birds that depend on these habitats for their survival and many of those are waders.

Part way through our travelling though we came across the encouraging story of the hooded plover in Australia. This gave us some hope and a realisation that actually there is something we can all do to mitigate some of the effects of the aforementioned problems. We started to raise money for BirdLife Australia to support the beach nesting birds programme of which the hooded plover was a beneficiary. To all intents and purposes, this programme is carried out by local volunteers on the beaches where the plovers were trying to breed. Simple and inexpensive measures were put into place along with many volunteer hours and within six years the breeding success of these attractive and endangered birds had increased tenfold from five per cent to fifty per cent; not perfect, but certainly a great improvement.

This we saw as the way forward. If each nest or roost site that needs protection can be cared for, not by the large organisations (which for administrative, financial and logistical reasons cannot be there for every beach and every nest) but by the people who live in the vicinity then surely these successes can be repeated across the planet. This concept we call Community Wader Conservation; local people protecting and nurturing local birds. Another fine example of this has been seen to work exceptionally well in North America where the previously Endangered piping plover is now Near Threatened, the threat level reduced, almost entirely, due to the efforts of local volunteers backed by Audubon.

Whilst those two projects are lucky to have the backing of conservation organisations, not every situation is so fortunate. Indeed the lady in the Netherlands, Astrid Kant, who we mentioned in chapter two, has been working with local farmers for nearly thirty years off her own bat, with no support whatsoever, to help save black-tailed godwit chicks from meadow mowing, which is occurring earlier each year.

With all this in mind we thought that perhaps an organisation that was dedicated to supporting and championing these small and localised conservation efforts, at the same time highlighting the problems to a wider audience, would have a place in the conservation network.

This then is what Wader Quest has become, a charity dedicated to supporting small conservation and research projects wherever they happen to be in the world. With regard to research projects, whilst we do not fund research projects simply because they involve waders, we are open to supporting those that are directly studying the effects of the local human population at wader breeding, stop over and wintering sites that also have an eye on involving the local population as part of that research. We greatly encourage projects that establish and foster an interest and pride within the local community in the waders, and their much threatened habitat, around them.

Wader Quest is an entirely voluntary organisation so we can guarantee that one hundred per cent of any donation, Corporate Sponsorship or Friends of Wader Quest subscription is put into a reserve fund and used exclusively for wader conservation. We rely entirely on the goodwill of people who care about what is unfolding around the world. People who are determined that our future generations will be able to witness the wonderful spectacle created by inspirations of wintering waders over our mud flats, enjoy the incredibly heart-warming sight of an adult bird tending to its ridiculously cute offspring, and to experience the magical sounds of moorlands, estuaries and other wild places that waders, of all kinds, enhance by their presence.

For further details of Wader Quest and our activities go to www.waderquest.org.

Bibliography

Allsop, Kenneth: *Adventure Lit Their Star* (1962)

Bayliss Smith, S.: *British Waders and their Haunts* (1950)

Bosworth, Fred: *The Last of the Curlews* (1954)

Brandt, Herbert: *Alaskan Bird Trails* (1943)

Brontë, Emily: *Wuthering Heights* (1847)

Brown, Leslie: *Birds and I* (1947)

Brown, P. E.: *Avocets in England* (1950)

Byrkjedal, Ingvar & Des Thompson: *Tundra Plovers* (1998)

Chandler, Richard J.: *Shorebirds in Action* (2017)

Chandler, Richard J.: *Shorebirds of the Northern Hemisphere* (2009)

Clare, Horatio: *Orison for a Curlew* (2017)

Cocker, Mark & Richard Mabey: *Birds Brittanica* (2005)

Cocker, Mark: *Birds and People* (2013)

Colwell, Mary: *Curlew Moon* (2018)

Cramer, Deborah: *The Narrow edge* (2015)

Cramp, Stanley & K. E. L. Simmons: *Handbook of the Birds of Europe the Middle East and North Africa. The Birds of the Western Palearctic* Vol. III – Waders to Gulls (1993)

del Hoyo, Josep, Andrew Elliot & Jordi Sargatal: *Handbook of the Birds of the World – Vol. 3* (1996)

Dixon, Charles: *Annals of Bird* Life (1890)

Dixon, Charles: *Curiosities of Bird Life* (1897)

Elliot, Daniel Giraud: *North American Shorebirds* (1893)

Ennion, E. A. R.: *The Lapwing* (1949)

Fjeldså, Jon: *Guide to the Young of European Precocial Birds* (1977)

Gooders, John: *Birds That Came Back* (1983)

Gray, Jeannie & Ian Fraser: *Australian Bird Names: A Complete* Guide (2013)

Greenoak, Francesca: *All the Birds of the* Air (1979)

Groundwater, William: *The Birds and Mammals of Orkney* (1974)

Hammond, Nicholas & Bruce Pearson: *Waders Behaviour Guide* (1994)

Hayman, Peter, John Marchant & Tony Prater: *Shorebirds - An identification guide to the waders of the world* (1986)

Hill, David: *Turner's Birds—Bird Studies from Farnley Hall* (1988)

Hirschfeld, Eric, Andy Swash & Rob Still: *The Worlds rarest Birds* (2013)

Hollands, David & Clive Minton: *Waders. The Shorebirds of Australia* (2012)

Hoose, Phillip: *Moonbird. A year on the wind with the great survivor B95* (2012)

Hosking, Eric & C. Newberry: *Intimate Skethces from Bird Life* (1945)

Hudson, Robert: *Threatened Bird of Europe* (1975)

Jobling, James A.: *Helm Dictionary of Scientific Bird Names* (2010)

Johns, Rev. C. A.: *British Birds in their Haunts* (1893)

Johns, Rev. C. A.: *British Birds in their Haunts* - Revised by J. A. Owen 12th Edition (1938)

Johnson, Oscar W. & Susan Scott: *Hawai'i's Kōlea* (2016)

Kant, Astrid *Weidvogels* (2011)

Kirkman, F.B. & Horace G. Hutchinson: *British Sporting Birds* (1924)

Landsborough Thomson, A. (Ed): *A New Dictionary of Birds* (British Ornithologists' Union) (1965)

Lappo, Elena, Pavel Tomkovich & Evgeny Syroechkovskiy: *Atlas of Breeding Waders in the Russian Arctic* (2012)

Lloyd, Karen: *Curlew Calling An Anthology of Poetry, Nature Writing and Images in Celebration of Curlew* (2017)

Loyd, Lewis R. W.: *Bird Facts and Fallacies* (1934?)

Mattheissen, Peter: *The Wind Birds* (1973)

Merritt, Matt: *A Sky Full of Birds* (2016)

Nares,Robert: *A glossary; or, a collection, of words, phrases, names and allusions to custom, proverbs &c. which have been thought to require illustration in the works of English authors particularly Shakespeare and his contemporaries* (1822)

Nethersole-Thompson, Desmond: *The Dotterel* (1973)

Nethersole-Thompson, Desmond & Maime: *Waders in their Breeding Haunts and Watchers* (1986)

Nichols, J. C. M.: *Birds of Marsh and Mere - and how to shoot them* (1926)

O'Brien, Michael, Richard Crossley & Kevin Karlson: *The Shorebird Guide* (2006)

Palin, Steve: *A Dissimulation of Birds - Illustrated Collective Nouns of Birds* (1998)

Peacock, Faansie: *Waders* (2016)

Pearse, Theed: *Birds of the Early Explorers in the Northern Pacific* (1968)

Piersma, Theunis & Jan van de Kam: *Marathon Migrants* (2016)

Pollard, Hugh B. C. & Frank Southgate.: *Wildfowl and Waders – Nature and Sport in the Coastlands* (1928)

Prater, A. J., J. H. Marchant & J. Vuorinen: *Guide to the Identification & Ageing of Holarctic Waders* (1997)

Reedman, Ray: *Lapwings, Loons & Lousy Jacks* (2016)

Richmond, Kenneth: *Birds of Britain* (1962)

Robertson, Hugh A. (Ed.): *Wader Studies in New Zealand*: Notornis various authors (1999)

Seth-Smith, David: *Birds of our Country & of the Dominions, Colonies and Dependencies.* Vol II T-Y

Shrubb, Michael: *Feasting, Fowling and Feathers* (2013)

Shrubb, Michael: *The Lapwing* (2007)

Sick, Helmut: *Birds in Brazil* (1993)

Simpson, Rick & Elis Simpson: *Eury the Spoon-billed Sandpiper* (2016)

Skelton, John: *The Book of Phillip Sparrow* (before 1508)

Slater, Rev. Henry H.: *British Birds with their Nests and Eggs* Vol. V pp53-178 (1893)

Snow, D. W. & C. M. Perrins: *The birds of the Western Palearctic Consise Edition* Vol 1.(1998)

Thiselton-Dyer, Thomas Firminger: *English Folk Lore* (1878)

W. G. Hale: *Waders* (1980

Threlfo, Glen: *Sharing a Dream* (1985)

van Rhijn, Johan G.: *The Ruff* (1991)

Vaughan, Richard: *Arctic Summer* (1979)

Vaughan, Richard: *In Search of Arctic Birds* (1992)

Vaughan, Richard: *Plovers* (1980)

Vaurie, Charles: *The birds of the Palearctic Fauna – Non Passerines* (1965)

Vesey-Fitzgerald, Brian: *A Book of British Waders* (1939)

Vesey-Fitzgerald, Brian: *British Game* (1946)

Whymper, Charles: *Egyptian Birds Painted and Described By Charles Whymper* (1909)

Wolley, John. (Ed. Alfred Newton): *Ootheca Wolleyana - An illustrated catalogue. The Collection of Birds' Eggs* Vol.II (1905-1907)

Woodley, Keith: *Godwits – Long-haul Champions* (2009)

Woodley, Keith: *Shorebirds of New Zealand—Sharing the margins* (2012)

Other reference titles

Complete Works of William Shakespeare

Guinness Book of World Records

Journals and periodicals

British Birds – British Birds Rarities Committee

Global Flyway Network newsletter – Global Flyway Network.

Hana Hou! - Hawaiian Airline Magazine

Tattler Newsletter - Asia Pacific Flyways

Wader Quest the newsletter – Wader Quest

Wader Study Group Bulletin / Wader Study – International Wader Study Group

Ibis - British Ornithological Union

<u>Papers and Articles</u>

Glegg , W. E.: *The Folklore of Birds in Relation to Essex.* Essex
Naturalist Vol. XXVII: 1940-46.
Hadden, Don W.: *Birds of the northern atolls of the North Solomons
Province of Papua New Guinea.* Notornis 51(2): 91–102 (2004)
Johnsgard, Paul A.: *Where Have All the Curlews Gone?* August 1980

<u>Websites</u>

Birdlife Australia
Birdlife International Species factsheets - www.birdlife.org
British Trust for Ornithology (BTO) - www.bto.org
East Asian-Australasian Flyways Partnership (EAAFP) -
www.eaaflyway.net
Euring - euring.org
Hansard Online hansard.parliament.uk
Indiana Division of Fish & Wildlife - www.in.gov
International Wader Study Group - www.waderstudygroup.org/
Internet Bird Collection - ibc.lynxeds.com
New Zealand Birds *Nga Manu o Aotearoa* - www.nzbirds.com
Oiseaux.net - www.oiseaux.net
Royal Society for the Protection of Birds (RSPB) - www.rspb.org.uk
Wader Quest – www.waderquest.org

Index

Act, 1981 Wildlife and Countryside: 78
Agrippa, Cornelius: 55
aidhircleog: 70
'*Akekeke*: 64
Allsop, Kenneth: 44
Amandan-Mòintich: 61
Athena: 56
Audubon, John James: 36
avocet: 118
    pied: 81,102
B95: 95-97
Baker, Dr. Allan: 17
batuira-do-banda: 116
baueri: 91-94
Beaver, Sir Hugh: 84
Bianki, Vitaly: 15
Bill,
    1926 Wild Bird Protection: 78
    1928 Protection of Lapwing: 78
Bird Club,
    Cambridgeshire: 82
    Fylde: 82
    Glamorgan: 83
    Huddersfield: 83
    Isle of Mull: 82
    Ogston: 82
    Peterborough: 82
    Wirral: 82
Bird Group, Swillington Ings: 82
Birdwatching Society,
    Lancaster and District: 82
    Wensum Valley: 82
Bodsworth, Fred: 43
Bond Friese VogelWachten: 79
Bottomley, Brian and Sheila: 23
Bride: 70
Brigid: 70
British Trust for Ornithology (BTO):

4,21,23,101
Britten, Benjamin: 38
Brönte, Emily: 40,41
Brueghel, Jan The Elder: 35
Bush, George W.: 85-86
Calidris canutus piersmai: 11
Camden, William: 63
Caxton, William: 40
Chandler, Richard: 22
Charadrius: 52
Chaucer, Geoffrey: 40
chewsit: 41
chorlito: 61
clam: 72-73
Clare,
    Horatio: 44
    John: 41,53
Clark, Nigel: 4
Clay,
    George: 16
    Rob: 16-17
Collective noun: 107-111, 115-122
Columbus, Christopher: 67-68
Colwell, Mary: 23-25
Cook,
    Capt. James: 69
    J. M.: 51
Council, Wirral Borough: 27,29,30
courser, double-banded: 6
Covenanters: 58
crow: 115
Curlew: 37
curlew,
    Eskimo: 43,68,70
    Eurasian: 23,24,25,27,38,42,66, 67,83,102,117
    little: 3,83
    slender-billed: 4,44

Daedalus: 56
Dee Estuary Voluntary Wardens (DEVW): 27,28,29,30
de Saint Hilaire, Geoffrey: 50
dix-huit: 53
dotterel,
    Eurasian: 61-62,64,116
dotterell: 61
dove: 85
Drayton Michael: 41
Dryden, John: 56
dunlin: 27,28,102,110,119
E7: 92-94
Easter Bunny: 57,58
English Nature: 27
Ennion, Eric: 20,21
Eostre: 57
Festival,
    Adelaide Shorebird: 30
    Copper Delta Shorebird: 29
    de Aves Playeras Bahia San Antonio: 19,30
    de Aves Playeras Puerto Rico
    de Aves Playeras Rio Gallego: 30
    Gray's Harbor Shorebird: 29
    Horseshoe Crab abd Shorebird: 29
    Jamaica Bay Shorebird: 29
    Kachemak Bay Shorebird: 29
    Oregon Shorebird: 29
    Severn Wader: 30
    Tofino Shorebird: 29
    Walney Wader: 30
    Wash Wader: 30
    Wirral Wader: 30
Flint, Prof. Vladimir: 15
Friedrich, Caspar David: 36
Gille-Bhrighde: 70
God: 59,117

godwit: 27,80,110,117
  bar-tailed: 91-94,102
  black-tailed: 13,14,15,37,82,102,
    117,134
goldcrest: 71-72
Golden Welly Award: 84
goldfinch: 115
González, Patricia: 17-19
Gould, John: 36
Gower, John: 40,56
Great Maker: 72
greenshank, common: 2,20
Groundwater, William: 58
Grove, Lucy: 42-3
Guinness
  Book of Records: 85
  Brewery: 84
  World Records: 85
guttersnipe: 121
Hadden, Don W.: 87
hare, European: 57
Hawaiian Airlines: 87-88
Hera: 54
Herod: 70
Herodotus: 49,50
hleapwince: 53
hoopoe: 56
Hunakai: 88
Jesus: 58,59,65,70
Kahuna: 63
Kakī: 100-101
Kamakawiwo'ole, Israel: 37
Kant, Astrid: 13-15,134
kievit: 53
killdeer: 85-86,116
King
  Canute: 42
  Charles II: 58
  of the Netherlands: 15
knot, red: 11,12,17,18,22,27,28,41,95
  -97,102,110,119
kō lea: 63-64,88
Koleamoku: 63
Lamia: 54
lapwing,
  northern: 1,5,6,33,34,35,36,
    38,40,41,52-58,60,70,77-
    79,80,82,110,115,132
  red-wattled: 60
  spur-winged: 50-51
Lapwings: 37
lark: 115
Leeming, Karen: 28
limpet: 73
ljip: 78
Lloyd, Karen: 42
Messiaen, Oliver: 37
Minton,
  Clive: 20-22,23
  Pat: 21
Moloka'i: 63
Moonbird: 17,95-96,102
morinellus: 61
Moses: 55
Mother Nature: 117
Museum,
  Natural History, London: 2
  Royal Ontario: 12

Zoological, Moscow State Uni.:
  16
naescus: 70
Nares, Robert: 53
Natural England: 28
nazongers: 79,80
Nottinghamshire Birdwatchers: 83
Ogham: 69-70
OG-YR: 94-95
Ornithological Club, North Cotswold
  and Bradford: 82
Ornithological Society,
  Banbury: 25
  Derbyshire: 82
  Gower: 82
  Shoreham District: 82
  South Cheshire: 82
Ovid: 56
owl, short-eared: 71
oystercatcher: 70,71,72,74,80,115,118,
  119
  Eurasian: 27,82,101
partridge: 56
peep: 119
peewit: 2,60
Pepys, Samuel: 119
Perdix: 57
peregrine: 119
pewet: 41
phalarope: 120,121
  grey: 22
  red-necked: 96-98
Philomela: 56
Piersma, Theunis: 11
pigeon: 61,110
  Passenger: 68
  Wood: 60
Ploeg, Syb van der: 37
Plover: 37,
plover: 52,61,65,94,110,115,116,121
  American golden: 17,68
  common ringed: 82,110,116
  Egyptian: 49-50
  European golden: 64,84
  golden plover: 65,66
  green: 2
  grey: 2,3,16,20,102,110
  hooded: 133
  Kentish: 50
  little ringed: 44,82
  mountain: 116
  Pacific golden: 63,68,88
  piping: 98-100,134
  semipalmated: 116
  shore: 94-95
  snowy: 116
plover's eggs: 77,81
pluvier à collier interompu: 50
polyplagktos: 54
prairie ghost: 116
Procne: 56
Project Godwit: 82
Queen of The Netherlands: 79
rabbit: 58
Rautavaara, Einojuhani (1928-2016):
  38
redshank: 80
  common: 2,21,27
  spotted: 21

Richards, Gov. Ann W.: 85-86
Rocky: 98-100
Royal Society for the Protection of
  Birds (RSPB): 29,30,81,82,83,84
Rubens, Peter Paul: 35
ruff: 20,120
Ruysdel, Salomon van: 35
Saint
  Beuno: 66
  Bride: 70-71
  Patrick: 66
sanderling: 3,18,20,21,22,88,110,119
sandpiper: 72,119
  Baird's: 119
  buff-breasted: 16,17
  common: 86-87
  Cooper's: 86
  Cox's: 86
  curlew: 86
  green: 16-17
  pectoral: 86
  purple: 22
  semipalmated: 117
  sharp-tailed: 15, 86
  solitary: 17
  spoon-billed: 4,37,44,83, 125-
    127,133
  stilt: 3
  western: 117
  white-rumped: 18,117
Scolopacid: 120
Scott,
  Peter: 21
  Sir Walter: 39
Scottish Prebyterians: 58
Seven Whistlers: 64-65
Shakespeare, William: 40
sheep: 110
Skelton, John: 61
snipe: 70,72-73,122
  common: 35,41,58,121
sniper: 122
Solomon: 56
Spangenberg, Eugeny: 15
sparrow: 63
starling, Eurasian: 110
stilt,
  black: 100-101
  black-winged: 83
  white-headed: 58,100
stint: 119
surfbird: 120
swift, common: 64
Talos: 56-57
tattler: 120
  wandering: 37,88
Tereus: 56
The Sandpipers: 37
The Shorebirds: 37
Thiselton-Dyer, Rev. Thomas
  Firminger: 65
thrush Swainson's: 3
Tomkovich, Pavel: 15
Turner,
  David: 25-27
  John: 34
turnstone, ruddy: 3,64,110
Tyrwhitts: 58
Twain, Mark: 121

'*Uhk*: 37,63-64,88
University,
    Groningen: 11
    Moscow State: 15,16
Vanellus: 41
Verkuil, Yvonne: 11-13
Wader Ringing Group, Wash: 101
Wader Study Group,
    Australian: 22
    Humber: 25
    International (IWSG): 11,13,25
    Victoria: 22
Ward, Jake: 38

Welch, Jemma: 100
Wetland Bird Survey (WeBS): 28
whaup: 66
Whimbrel: 37
whimbrel,
    Eurasian: 64,65,66,83,102
    little: 3,83
Western Hemisphere Shorebird
    Reserve Network (WHSRN): 16
Wildfowl and Wetlands Trust
    (WWT): 4,5,24,30,82
Wildlife Trust,
    Cheshire: 30

Cumbria: 30
Williams, Helen Maria: 39
Wolley, John: 52
woodcock,
    American: 72
    Eurasian: 34,71-72,102,122
Woodpigeon: 59
Wordsworth, William: 65
writing birds: 120
wrybill: 95
Yeats, W. B.: 39
yellowlegs: 122
Zeus: 54-55